New Latitudes
Theory and English Renaissance Literature

Thomas Healy

Lecturer in English, Birkbeck College,
University of London

Edward Arnold
A division of Hodder & Stoughton
LONDON   MELBOURNE   AUCKLAND

© 1992 Thomas Healy

First published in Great Britain 1992

Distributed in the USA by Routledge, Chapman and Hall, Inc.
29 West 35th Street, New York, NY 10001

British Library Cataloguing in Publication Data

Healy, Thomas
  New latitudes: Theory and English Renaissance Literature
  I. Title
  820.1

ISBN 0-340-49308-9

Typeset in 11/12pt Linotron Palatino by
Hewer Text Composition Services, Edinburgh
Printed in Great Britain for Edward Arnold,
a division of Hodder and Stoughton Limited,
Mill Road, Dunton Green, Sevenoaks, Kent TN13 2YA by
St Edmundsbury Press, Bury St Edmunds, Suffolk
and bound by Hartnolls Ltd, Bodmin, Cornwall

for Margaret

Contents

A Note on the Texts

This book is primarily designed for those new to the study of English Renaissance texts and culture and for those seeking to familiarise themselves with some of the current critical debates within that study. I have, as far as possible, used editions of texts which readers are likely to possess or have easy access to, rather than standard scholarly editions which can be consulted only by a small number in a position to use well-provisioned libraries. Quotations from Shakespeare are taken from the one-volume Alexander edition (London, Collins, 1951); from Spenser's *The Faerie Queene*, ed. Thomas P. Roche Jr (Harmondsworth, Penguin, 1978); from Milton *Complete English Poems, Of Education, Areopagitica*, ed. Gordon Campbell (London, J. M. Dent, 1990).

Preface

Why examine English Renaissance literature? This may seem a strangely innocent, even naive question to ask, betraying a number of critical suppositions which need interrogating. What is meant by literature? Does literature imply a privileging of certain generic forms of writing over other types we might read? Does literature consist only of those forms of writing traditionally defined as 'serious' and should they be considered separately from other forms of writing? Further, what is meant by Renaissance? Is it a span of years, specific cultural preoccupations, a collection of discourses formed in the present and applied to written artefacts of the past, or all of the above? Does Renaissance imply distinct cultural phenomena and how do we constitute the culture that the Renaissance represents? Are there definable *Renaissance* preoccupations which can be separated from other cultural practices which occurred at the same time? Additionally, should we not ask who 'we' are? Is there a constituency of willing general readers in the 1990s for a Renaissance text? Is not a likely answer to why we examine Renaissance texts, 'Because we have to'? Current readers of the Renaissance are probably students and teachers, part of institutional processes that have prescribed that 'we' examine and are examined in Renaissance writing.

Seeking among those currently working in Renaissance studies for answers to these questions and similar ones about why we examine Renaissance texts will elicit very different responses from those of the recent past. Many of the questions posed above would have seemed inappropriate fifteen or twenty years ago. It would have largely been passively assumed that the Renaissance's literary qualities were so manifest ('the Golden Age of English writing'!) and the general cultural character of the period so widely established, that every right-thinking educated person would acknowledge what the Renaissance was and the reasons for examining it. A critical establishment selected texts and analysed them within methodologies and critical languages which supported propositions about the period's self-evident qualities.

We now recognise much greater diversity and pluralism in how we undertake constructions of cultural identity and how we analyse the character of literary texts. The changes in our explorations of literary texts which have resulted from engagements with new theoretical ideas during the last decade have made both the questions that we ask of texts and the answers they provide us with increasingly problematic. There are contending voices asking us to consider our experience of all writing in a large variety of ways. Our critical practice has lost its innocence. This is a good thing; but it also makes our critical activities more demanding because we confront a host of issues which traditional literary study ignored. Perhaps most emphatically, theory has insisted we become aware of our positions as critics. To the question: 'What is this text saying?', we must add 'Why do I think it is speaking in the way it does?' and 'Why am I adopting a particular methodology for examination rather than another?' There are really no questions we can ask which do not have theoretical implications and none which do not insist on rigorous self-scrutiny of our motives and desires in reading the Renaissance the way we do.

I believe that writing in England from the early sixteenth until the mid-seventeenth century sufficiently reveals many of the same preoccupations (social, cultural, political) and uses the same generic resources for representing them to allow some collective considerations of its output. The problems of creating categories is that such organisations resist those objects and discourses which cannot be neatly incorporated into them. But categories also allow us to discover possibilities of significances in texts which would otherwise remain unknown. The need, ideally, is to discover categories which admit alternatives, allowing the fullest range of significances in texts to be uncovered.

I decided to write this book because I am acutely aware that the type of critical questions I want to ask of Renaissance texts in the 1990s are very different from the ones I asked a decade ago. Yet, as a lecturer in a university involved in teaching English literary writing during the early modern period (about 1500 to 1660), I constantly find that my students have expectations of this period's writing which suggest that the impact of recent critical debates focused on the Renaissance is not reaching them. It is not that they are opposed to new theoretical concerns. Some will be quite happy to engage with a sophisticated analysis of gender in late-nineteenth-century novels, or struggle with post-structuralist readings of Joyce. But when it comes to studying the Renaissance, too many seem to assume that the critical dynamism which enlivens discussions of nineteenth- and twentieth-century texts is missing and, even worse, not really appropriate when considering early modern writing. The implication seems to be that the Renaissance is 'heritage', at best something academically interesting but remote, divorced from the concerns within writing they wish to confront. I hope this book will make a small contribution to changing this attitude.

There is another group I also wish to address. Those who come to the Renaissance with an appetite for engaging in the critical debates taking place within Renaissance studies only to be confronted by a huge range of specialist studies with which it is difficult for those new to the period to negotiate. There have been some excellent books and collections of essays which have helped non-specialist readers with major authors, notably Shakespeare.[1] There have been important accessible studies directed at specific areas of cultural concern, such as Lisa Jardine's or Kathleen McLuskie's work on women and drama.[2] But there has also been an increasing tendency for many critics to assume a specialist professional audience familiar with the ground, acquainted through patient reading in well-stocked libraries with both Renaissance texts and the critical enterprises that have grown up around them. One of the characteristics of recent theory's impact on our study of the Renaissance has been a wariness among critics to make large generalised claims. The scholarly essay rather than

[1] See for instance John Drakakis (ed.) *Alternative Shakespeares* (London, Methuen, 1985); Jonathan Dollimore and Alan Sinfield (eds). *Political Shakespeare: New Essays in Cultural Materialism* (Manchester, Manchester University Press, 1985); Kiernan Ryan, *Shakespeare* (Hemel Hempstead, Harvester Wheatsheaf, 1989).
[2] Lisa Jardine, *Still Harping on Daughters: Women and Drama in the Age of Shakespeare* (Brighton, Harvester, 1983); Kathleen McLuskie, *Renaissance Dramatists* (Hemel Hempstead, Harvester Wheatsheaf, 1989).

the monograph is the favoured form. Books often take the form of a number of linked and not-so-linked essays, many of which have circulated already in journals. Intellectually, of course, there is nothing wrong with this. But a profusion of specialist, fragmented studies is one of the difficulties those unfamiliar with recent critical developments have to surmount.

What I hope to accomplish with this book is to offer a short introduction to some of the major critical preoccupations found in debates about Renaissance English literature during the last fifteen years or so. The book is designed either for those who have only recently embarked on examining Renaissance texts or for those who feel puzzled by some of the recent critical debates which have been focused around texts they may be long familiar with. Renaissance texts are exciting both as repositories of vanished cultural practices and as empowered writing which can help us to clarify and more clearly address our own cultural needs. Recent literary and cultural theory has helped us to explore Renaissance texts in the historicity of their own moments of production and in the negotiated moments of their cultural reception until the present. If I can entice a few readers to see new possibilities in the Renaissance, I will be well satisfied with my work.

Theory is a vast field. It is not a unified field as some of its opponents like to imagine, but contains the possibilities of a huge plurality of critical methodologies. Many of these are opposed and contradictory. Most critics working in any area of critical concern recognise that it is entirely possible to read texts differently by employing another methodology. This is not to suggest texts can mean anything. It does mean they can mean different things in different critical projects. Our examination of the past is undertaken within the structures of a large number of different centres of concern. The possibilities and organisation of significances contained within any text will depend on the critical encodings through which the text is perceived. Most critical writers within Renaissance studies recognise critical pluralism and feel it to be one of the positive benefits conferred by a greater theoretical awareness. But a recognition of potential plurality of meanings does not prevent assumptions within critical practice that some meanings are more significant than others or that some critical methodologies are preferable to others. One of the most widely and bitterly articulated debates in the last decade has been between those who feel literary theory is best kept separate from history, and those who feel history and theory are inseparably combined.[1]

As will be clear in the following chapters, it is the latter view which I favour. As will also be clear, I make no pretence of trying to write some form of balanced encyclopaedia-style account which tries to allow all the different critical voices currently found in Renaissance studies equal coverage on their own terms. I have tried to pick out a wide range of areas where critical debates about Renaissance texts are focused, but I recognise that there are others. I have indicated where I believe the most significant work has been done, some of the problems which it raises and some directions I see criticism taking, but I have avoided trying to reduce complex issues to easily applied labels. Though the chapters are arranged so that one critical focus is usually under consideration in each, it will be recognised that many of the critical areas of concern overlap. In general, I have aimed to produce a readable short book rather than one which tried to squeeze too much in.

Some introductions to theory and literature attempt to keep the two separate. They will outline the ideas of particular theorists and then suggest how they might be applied in reading texts. Generally, I have not attempted this. Rather, I have tried to concentrate on how theoretical ideas may be seen to influence our understanding of different types of texts and of different ways of understanding Renaissance culture. Whatever their origins, most theoretical ideas become modified and transformed as they are debated and deployed, so that it does not seem particularly useful to try to return them to their originators. I am not really interested in outlining genealogies of critical methodologies. I am more interested in showing readers how theoretical practices can be seen working in exploring

[1] See J. Hillis Miller, 'Presidential Address 1986. The triumph of theory, the resistance to reading and the question of the material base', *PMLA*, 102 (1987), pp. 281–91. For a rejoinder with a specifically Renaissance context: Louis A. Montrose, 'Professing the Renaissance: the poetics and politics of culture' in H. Aram Veeser (ed.), *The New Historicism* (New York: Routledge, 1989), pp. 15–36.

Renaissance texts, hoping to entice them to attempt their own.

As is discussed in Chapter 3, one impact of recent theory has been to encourage readers to look outside a narrowly prescribed literary canon of Renaissance texts. I discuss throughout this book the importance of thinking about areas of writing which have previously been ignored and try to indicate what some of these areas and texts are. Yet, I am very aware of the practical difficulties of many readers in gaining access to such material. As a result, I have centred my discussions on those texts which most students have ready access to and which are likely to be the ones they encounter in most current courses. I hope this will allow most readers to test and challenge some of this book's ideas.

I could not have imagined completing this book without the intellectual support of two groups engaged in debating many of the issues which appear here: the London Renaissance Seminar and the Graduate Theory Seminar at Birkbeck College. I particularly acknowledge my debts to Lorna Hutson, Lisa Jardine, Tony Parr, Jonathan Sawday, Sabina Sharkey and Susan Wiseman of the London Renaissance Seminar and to Isobel Armstrong, Helen Carr, Steven Connor, Laura Marcus and Carol Watts of the Graduate Theory Seminar. I would no less warmly like to acknowledge the help of many other colleagues, notably Gordon Campbell, Robert Clark, Sandra Clark, Barbara Hardy, James Knowles, Kate McLuskie, Robert Miles, and Stan Smith. Over the past years, students at Birkbeck College have helped focus some of the book's arguments and, often unknowingly, offered a large number of valuable contributions to its substance. I should like especially to thank Wendy Amy-Chinn, David Atter, Diane Davies, and Chris Shaldon. Sabina Sharkey and Susan Wiseman read chapters, offering insights and saving me from some significant errors. Christopher Wheeler at Edward Arnold has been an ideal editor, indeed the idea for the volume was to a large extent his. Margaret Healy, as always, has proved my greatest support and my most exacting reader. The faults that remain, of course, are my own.

1
Past and Present

In the preface of his book *The Elizabethan World Picture*, E.M.W.Tillyard stated his book's intention as being:

> to extract and expound the most ordinary beliefs about the constitution of the world as pictured in the Elizabethan age and through this exposition to help the ordinary reader to understand and to enjoy the great writers of the age.[1]

The dominant ruling idea of Renaissance England Tillyard found was the belief in a cosmic order which governed both human institutions and natural phenomena. *The Elizabethan World Picture* appeared in 1943 during a period when many feared for the collapse of western civilisation. The values and ideals believed to underlie Anglo-Saxon institutions appeared threatened and unstable. A rallying point was needed and, for Tillyard, one was found in the golden age of the Elizabethan world. Here was a period when a universally accepted order could be discovered with a resulting social and political stability. Tillyard suggested the principle of order was so taken for granted by the age that it was rarely directly articulated – 'the utter commonplaces too familiar for the poets to make detailed use of except in explicitly didactic passages, but essential as basic assumptions and invaluable at moments of high passion'.[2] By recalling the strength of these beliefs and the cultural, especially literary, achievements this order produced, the Anglo-Saxon world could see more clearly the common need to defend those essential characteristics of its civilisation against the barbarous foe.

Similarly, Sir Laurence Olivier's wartime film of Shakespeare's *Henry V* (1944), where the King rallies the hopelessly outnumbered English army on the night before Agincourt with the rhetoric of religious-nationalism, was

---

[1] E. M. W. Tillyard, *The Elizabethan World Picture* (Harmondsworth, Penguin, 1963), p. 8.
[2] Ibid., p. 7.

clearly Olivier speaking for England in a moment of wartime crisis. The film was prominently dedicated to the paratroop and airborne divisions. The Elizabethan world provided the model and supplied the language for a present national need. The film opens with a bird's-eye view of an ideally represented, prosperous, clean London. The camera then descends to an idyllically landscaped south bank and presents a Globe Theatre where all classes (both women and men) happily gather to hear the play. Certainly, these are different physical circumstances than would have confronted the Renaissance theatre-goer, but more notably the film's scenic panorama provokes a staggeringly glaring comparison with the perspectives offered by a blitzed London outside the cinema. The production itself carefully suppresses those aspects of Shakespeare's play which suggest that Henry's endeavours are not somehow the shared desires of the nation – most notably it cuts out any mention of the English traitors in Act II. In the context of the early 1940s (Olivier's film was conceived in 1941 before America had formally joined in the war) this creation of an idealised Elizabethan past was particularly convenient for Britain trying to persuade America to participate wholeheartedly in the war effort for the preservation of civilisation against barbarism. Elizabethan England could be portrayed as a period before emigration to the Amerian colonies began, before the ruptures between a British and American way of life existed. Ignoring the complex racial and national make-up of Americans, the attempt was to offer Elizabethan England as a time before Americans had 'left' their home culture. It was as much their world as it was ours, and the recollection of other less co-fraternal moments such as 1776 or 1812 were displaced by these representations of shared origins.

I do not mean to suggest that Tillyard or Olivier simply undertook their tasks as part of some officially orchestrated propaganda. They conceived that what they represented was accurate: *Henry V* as a play genuinely celebrating the national character, the Elizabethans were imagined as believing in a stable world order. What we can see, though, is that critical enterprises or cultural reproductions are not undertaken by disinterested participants removed from the concerns of their own historic moment. Tillyard engages

with the mid-twentieth century as he does with the sixteenth and early seventeenth centuries. As is apparent with
the *Henry V* film's cuts and remodelling of the Shakespeare
play, however, desires within the twentieth century mean
that aspects of the Renaissance which do not conform with
current needs are rendered silent.

Critical attention on the Renaissance during the 1980s
and now the 1990s is no more disinterested than during
the 1940s or at any other period. Criticism cannot see
its role as 'putting right' previous errors as though academic study was part of a stream of emendation aimed
at achieving some final truth about texts. Certainly, I do
not pretend any scholarly disinterest with this book. Like
many, I am uneasy about many current directions of our
civilisation. I would not for a moment propose we face
the same immediate peril confronting the world in the
early 1940s. My concerns are much more involved with
the dangers I perceive that many valued institutions are
having to confront within current political climates. Those
involved with the study of English are acutely aware of
the attacks on institutions of higher education in Britain,
in the rest of Europe, and in America during the past
decade which have caused activities within the humanities
to come under threat. One prominent German academic
proposed recently that, in reorganising higher education
after German unification, former East Germans should
'forget about the arts'.[1] The state's increasing insistence,
for example, that what people study and how they study it
are of government concern and to be directed at ends which
a government finds acceptable is part of the character of our
critical environment. This environment provokes the type
of inquiries we make of the past.

What is immediately striking is how most current studies
of Renaissance culture have found the reverse of Tillyard.
Where he found order, many now find disorder, or anxiety
about order. Where he projected an agreed consensus
among Elizabethans as to what the world picture consisted
of, we now discover contention and subversion. Where
he imagined a basic critical agreement among Renaissance
specialists as to what the 'relevant commonplaces' of the

[1] Reported in *The Times Higher Education Supplement*, 28 December 1990, 'Review of the
Year', p. viii.

period were, we now perceive no such agreement. Indeed, a mistrust about historical periods possessing common-places other than those selected and organised by critical inquiry undertaken for specific, if frequently unconscious, ideological ends is now the familiar assumption. This reversal of Tillyard's contentions reflects the unease which our present critical environment reveals about the world, past and present, that it engages with. Our experience of the way modern states exert control, restrict expression, manipulate language, has prompted us to search the past to see what similarities and differences existed from our own experience. This is not an exercise in self-indulgence. Since our experience of institutions is frequently other than the idealistic way they strive to represent themselves, the solidity of values apparently inherited from the past are called into question. It is appropriate to try to discover if such institutions were ever actually the way they had been previously presented by a scholarship interested (even if it did not declare its interest) in constructing its own version of the past to answer its own preoccupations. It is not surprising to find topics such as censorship, subversion, the conditions of patronage, power and authority, and the nature of individual identity at the centre of much recent critical enquiry into the Renaissance.

It is important to perceive that our interest in the past will be dictated by our involvement in the present. The notion of a superior disinterested scholarship intent upon objec-tivity is mythic. The pursuit of objectivity curiously results in a far more ideologically partial and subjective critical representation. Self-examination of critical motivation can actually allow some of the more tempting ideological dis-tortions we may feel inclined to pursue as 'truths' to be given a more accurate focus, to reveal their partiality to the reader. But we should certainly not mistrust or feel the need to apologise for pursuing the past because of the present. Tillyard's belief that Elizabethan literature could provide an encouragement in countering a threat to civili-sation may now seem naive and intellectually misplaced, but within the context of its origins it is not something we should immediately deride. Nor should a partiality in our present preoccupations with the English Renaissance be objected to. Our current cultural experience has revealed that the premise of a grand historical narrative presenting a unified cultural progression centred on interests that are male and European, and only dealing with activities engaged in by the minority in social and political control, can no longer compel our assent. We have become aware of other contending histories previously rendered largely invisible, such as women's history and the 'history from below' of groups socially disenfranchised by reason of class, colour, religion. One of the critical directions supported by recent work on the Renaissance is to render these other histories more visible and to examine the means by which they were hidden.

Literary texts are not some static crystalline structure in which we may glimpse a captured immobile past. The critic is not some simple custodian of these museum texts whose task it is to keep the displays polished so their readers can see them in clear unreflected light. Our relation with literary texts is formed through a complex intersection of past and present, moments of reception as well as moments of production are of equal importance. Criticism reworks the relations of past and present, and at its best it does so dynamically, intervening in the past and the present to offer changed perspectives. The result should be an activity, an exchange between past text, critical representation, and reader's response.

One of the features which noticeably emerged in the 1980s was a struggle for control of the past, a confrontation primarily between those who perceive contemporary western civilisation as a triumph and those who question such a perspective. On one side is a reiteration of the Whiggish, teleological view of history which dominated the nineteenth century, demonstrating present western culture as the result of a continuous enlightenment and development of civilisation from the beginnings of the early modern period until the present. In opposition to this perspective are those sceptical of models which project the past as a type of organic whole, a unified continuity which is subject to a continuous explanatory narrative. In dealing with English Renaissance writing we find, on the one hand, a neo-conservative critical agenda which has appropriated the Tillyardian perspective, projecting a stable agreed world order occasionally buffeted but never

disrupted by alien forces. A world which produces a literature that, at its best, celebrates essential and transcendent
human qualities. This presentation of the past is designed
to demonstrate that, now as then, those who desire fundamental change are seeking instability, threatening western
values anchored in the supposedly natural evolution of
social and political order. On the other hand are those
who offer a more radical agenda to our study of the past.
These critics perceive the Elizabethan golden age as a
mythic construction of later ages and, in actuality, to have
been a fragmented, ruptured world, contending issues of
gender, politics, religion, and cultural value without any
consensus. They present a critical agenda involved in a
current cultural confrontation – questioning the ideological
partiality of a neo-conservative critical perspective, which
apparently refuses to confront the terms on which it asserts
its authenticity and which limits the range of cultural
artefacts it will admit as civilised discourse. To participate,
therefore, in a critical confrontation with the Renaissance is
to participate in current ideological and political struggles.
Students reading for an essay topic are forming a view of
the past which will mould their view of how the future
can be constructed. To undertake a critical reading which
is unconcerned with how it is intervening in the present
is a denial of intellectual responsibility.

How may we examine Milton's or Marvell's poetry in
relation to the events of the mid-seventeenth century?
On the surface, the question seems to be one open to an
answer, if we allow that literary texts do circulate in history.
But the question raises a host of subsequent questions, each
of which will help determine the structure and focus of
our answer. What, to begin with, do we call the events of
the mid-seventeenth century, for convenience the period
1640–60?[1] There are many titles currently in use, each
betraying an ideological disposition towards the period's
events: the Interregnum, the Great Rebellion, the English
Revolution, the Civil War. The first two reveal an essentially conservative, royalist agenda. The period is seen as

---

[1] See Annabel Patterson, 'The very name of the game: theories of order and disorder', in
Thomas Healy and Jonathan Sawday (eds), *Literature and the English Civil War* (Cambridge,
Cambridge University Press, 1990), pp. 21–37. My discussion of the consequences of
naming the period 1640–60 owes much to Patterson's discussion.

an hiatus in an otherwise consistent historical development, built around a gradual political and social evolution,
centred on the monarchy. The Great Rebellion at least
acknowledges that there were other rebellions, though
not as consequential, but rebellion is an extraordinarily
loaded term – implying unlawful, morally improper and
ultimately unwarranted action against legitimate authority.
The term's application to this period originates in the Earl of
Clarendon's *History of the Rebellion and Civil Wars in England*
produced by a Royalist during the Restoration to celebrate
those who 'opposed and resisted that torrent' – rebellion
being unqualifiedly equated with disorderly, uncontrolled
catastrophe.[1] In modern appellation both terms, Interregnum and rebellion, are employed to contain the period's
effect, to suggest it was an aberration, rectified with the
restoration of the monarchy in 1660 when the 'normal'
pattern of English historical evolution was also restored.
In contrast, English Revolution proposes a very different
set of assumptions, perceiving the events of the period as
a definite rupture in the structure of history, a breakdown
of the old order and the emergence of a new one. Many
advocates of the title 'revolution' see the period achieving a
positive result, liberating groups of people who had previously been kept 'voiceless' by political disenfranchisement.
A further difference arising from naming is indicated by
entitling the mid-seventeenth century the Civil War period.
This might appear on the surface the most neutral formulation – there were unarguably three distinct times
of battles in 1642–6, 1648, and 1650–1 – but it also
elides the establishment of parliamentary authority and
later Cromwell's Protectorate. It was not a twenty-year
period of formal civil conflict. Further, the term suggests
its user is indicating a type of political neutrality towards
the events, an indefinable right and wrong existing on both
sides of the conflict. Again, the term implies an essential
uniqueness to the period, a time of conflict marked out as
distinct from other periods of social, political and religious
fracture.

Many writing on the mid-seventeenth century at present

---

[1] Edward Hyde, Earl of Clarendon, Selections from *'The History of the Rebellion'* and
'The Life by Himself', Hugh Trevor-Roper (ed.) (London, 1978), pp. 1–2.

would legitimately claim that I have marked out these positions too exclusively. There are those who feel, for instance, that a revolution did take place but not one which achieved positive effects; or others who dispute the existence of an English revolution but who do not adhere to a neo-conservative interpretation of English history. What I wish to indicate here is the complex issues involved in establishing what to call historical events. The idea that there is somehow an easy 'historical background' to the study of culture is obviously absurd. In practical terms, we see that in studying a literary text we cannot go off and find some singular historical textbook which offers a straightforward, impartial presentation of 'what happened'.

With Milton and Marvell, both of whom supported Parliament and were employed by the state during the Commonwealth and Protectorate, we have instances of writers with direct political involvement in their times. How we colour that time will have a huge bearing on how we see their works in relation to the period. Take the example of Marvell's 'An Horatian Ode upon Cromwell's Return from Ireland'. Traditionally, literary criticism – which generally has supported the conservative idea of the period as a time of disruption and rebellion – has made out a case for the poem's balanced quality in praising both Cromwell and Charles I.[1] Marvell may have later been an employee of Cromwell's Latin Secretariat, but his poem shows an independent impartiality which avoids political commitment. The poet Marvell can thus be somehow separated from the political Marvell working to maintain the Interregnum's government. But under the impact of historians who stress the period's revolutionary quality, readings of Marvell's poem as a political document celebrating the success of Cromwell in a positive frame have gained momentum.[2] The recognition that Marvell can be seen responding idealistically to the new age, and

[1] Most notably Cleanth Brooks, 'Marvell's *Horatian Ode*', *English Institute Essays, 1946* (New York, 1947), pp. 127–58. For a current rebuttal, see David Norbrook 'Marvell's "Horatian Ode" and the politics of genre', *Literature and the English Civil War*, op. cit., pp. 147–69.
[2] Blair Worden, 'Andrew Marvell, Oliver Cromwell, and the Horatian Ode', in Kevin Sharpe and Steven Zwicker (eds), *Politics of Discourse: The Literature and History of Seventeenth Century England* (Berkeley, University of California Press, 1987), pp. 147–80; Norbrook, ibid.

partisanly aligning his poetry with Commonwealth and
Protectorate aspirations is a consequence of admitting the
enthusiasm many during the mid-seventeenth century felt
for revolutionary events which would, they believed, bring
a new order.

One consequence of recent trends, therefore, is that
literary critics have been forced to recognise that they have
had to become involved in issues of history formerly the
preserve of historians, and can no longer take history for
granted. History is not some unmediated story of events.
It is a construct, often a narrative, of interested parties who
seek to prove a thesis of how events have been shaped.[1] In
the case of the mid-seventeenth century we find groups of
current historians who share social and frequently explicit
political assumptions identifying themselves with right and
left, and often implicitly acknowledging that their own
political agendas dictate not only their naming of the past
but their unhappiness with opposing critical orientations.

A notable example is J. C. Davis's *Fear, Myth, and History: The Ranters and the Historians*.[2] The Ranters were a
group of extreme religious libertarians who believed that
God dwelt inside them as an inner light. As a result any
act was justifiable as long as it was performed with the
working of the spirit. In practice this meant that Ranters
were identified with activities outside socially accepted
boundaries, for example indulging in sexual licence, blasphemy and swearing. They had a brief existence from 1649
until 1651 and were constantly attacked by government.
Davis argues, though, that there was no coherent Ranter
movement. Rather he sees them as an embodiment of
the fears of seventeenth-century conservatives worried
about the extreme forms radical religious movements were
taking. For Davis, the Ranters, as a group, are largely constructed by twentieth-century Marxist historians, notably
Christopher Hill, intent on finding groups who can justify
their thesis of a revolution. For the historians of the left,
Davis concluded, the Ranters are an example of a necessary

[1] For two differing perspectives see Hayden White, *The Content of the Form: Narrative Discourse and Historical Representation* (Baltimore, Johns Hopkins University Press, 1987); Dominick LaCapra, *Rethinking Intellectual History: Texts, Contexts, Language* (Ithaca, Cornell University Press, 1983).
[2] J. C. Davis, *Fear, Myth and History: The Ranters and the Historians* (Cambridge, Cambridge University Press, 1986).

group, freed by the breakdown of social and political institutions and dynamically prepared to break with tradition.
The necessity of discovering such groups causes historians
of the left to invent what never was. Davis's claims have
met with many objections.[1] Christopher Hill had always
acknowledged that it was doubtful that there had been
a Ranter organisation and difficult to define what 'the
Ranters' as a group believed as opposed to individuals
whose views came to be labelled as Ranters.[2] Nigel Smith
in the introduction to his *A Collection of Ranter Writings
from the 17th Century* – a book offering good evidence of
highly individualistic writings which nevertheless share a
number of common characteristics – emphasises that the
term Ranter was one coined to refer to all those deemed
to have extreme opinions.[3] But, as Smith's collection testi-
fies, there is substantial evidence of radical millennial and
egalitarian solutions circulating during the period.

The debate about Ranters is an instance of some historians, essentially neo-conservative in outlook, portraying
themselves as historians of order contending against those
who, they see, as historians of disorder, with all this implies
about the historian's objective rather than objectivity within
a political world dominated in the 1980s, at least in Britain
and America, by neo-conservative values.[4] Whether we
call some individuals Ranters, others Levellers, Diggers,
Muggletonians, early Quakers and so forth and then
present them either as a type of 'lunatic fringe' to
mainstream developments or, as Hill eloquently puts it
in his *The World Turned Upside Down*: 'the attempts of
various groups of the common people to impose their
own solutions to the problems of their time, in opposition
to the wishes of their betters who had called them into
political action'[5] is a matter of current political alignment
and represents the way we wish to intervene in the present
as in the past.

[1] Perhaps most thoroughly by Edward Thompson, 'On the Rant', in Geoff Eley and
William Hunt (eds), *Reviving the English Revolution: Reflections and Elaborations on the Work
of Christopher Hill* (London, Verso, 1988), pp. 153–60.
[2] Christopher Hill, *The World Turned Upside Down: Radical Ideas During The English
Revolution* (Harmondsworth, Penguin Books, 1975), pp. 203–4.
[3] Nigel Smith (ed.), *A Collection of Ranter Writings from the 17th Century* (London, Junction
Books, 1983), pp. 7–38.
[4] See Paterson, 'The very name of the game', op. cit., p. 33.
[5] Hill, *The World Turned Upside Down*, op. cit., p. 13.

The question that began this examination of the mid-seventeenth century was how can we explore the relations of Milton's and Marvell's poetry to the period? Does it matter, though, for literary criticism whether the poetry was formed out of a period of rebellion or revolution? Traditionally, literary criticism has paid little attention to questions of precise historical contextualisation. To locate a text in a specific historical milieu was only the preoccupation of specialist scholarship. The volumes of the still popular *Pelican Guide to English Literature* which refer to the Renaissance are called *The Age of Shakespeare* and *From Donne to Marvell*, for example.[1] The titles themselves clearly announce a supposed concern with only literary values. But Shakespeare's central importance within Renaissance writing was not a contemporary phenomenon, rather the result of later critical judgements. How can the 'age' be called his? The *Guide*'s critical position assumes Shakespeare produced a body of autonomous work which reflected his uninhibited intentions, and this (unstated) supposition certainly pushes history to the background. Shakespeare's standing, as any other writer's, was imagined to be determined by an expression of values which transcended the historical moment. The *Pelican Guide* proposes that accounts of the social context of literature are included in the volumes to suggest the factors which merely *encouraged* forms of literary production.[2] Great literature comes to be imagined as the private, autonomous utterances of authors in a position to control their unfettered subjectivity regardless of historical constraint. This ignores, for instance, the fact that some of Shakespeare's plays were written during Elizabeth's reign and others during James I's, when political conditions changed and, as important, the terms of political representation differed (in which dramatic productions importantly figured).[3] Alert as we are now to the interaction between writing and history, we can perceive that it was certainly not Shakespeare's

---

[1] Boris Ford (ed.), *The Pelican Guide to English Literature*, 7 vols, (Harmondsworth, Penguin, 1955).
[2] Ibid. 'General Introduction', pp. 8–9.
[3] See for example, Jonathan Goldberg, *James I and the Politics of Literature: Jonson, Shakespeare, Donne and Their Contemporaries* (Baltimore, Johns Hopkins University Press, 1983).

'age'. His drama negotiates historical moments in which Shakespeare was not in control of the artistic, political or social conditions of the culture in which his writing was produced. Similarly, seventeenth-century literary history is not merely a progress of lyric development from Donne to Marvell.

p.131

For traditional criticism it did not make an especial difference whether the date of composition of Milton's *Samson Agonistes* was assigned to 1647–53 during the Civil War or to the Restoration period of 1660–70.[1] The historical circumstances of a text were important so that localised issues could be clarified and explained – effectively so they could be explained away. The issues in *Samson* were focused commonly on the internal struggles of the individual confronted with temptation, and whether the poem achieved a tragic dimension or not. In traditional critical study, questions about politics were rarely felt important since politics engaged with transitory activities. William Riley Parker's monumental biography of Milton, which appeared after a lifetime's research in 1968, resolutely portrays Milton's involvement with the politics of the mid-seventeenth century as an unfortunate distraction.[2] The prose which preoccupied Milton during the Commonwealth and Protectorate periods was to be seen as separate and certainly intrinsically less interesting than the poetry in which Parker portrays Milton participating in some universalised European humanism. From this critical position, Milton's poetry was thought to have no points of contact with the writing of the Ranters. Indeed Ranter writing was not thought to be a proper subject for literary inquiry.

The new insistence that a text's mediation in history is important has changed this perspective. Christopher Hill's *Milton and the English Revolution*[3] challenged the idea of a Milton primarily concerned to participate in an elite humanist culture. As Hill demonstrated, Miltonic

---

[1] For a discussion of the poem's date see John Carey (ed.), *John Milton: Complete Shorter Poems* (London, Longman, 1971), pp. 328–30. My discussion of *Samson Agonistes* is much indebted to Thomas N. Corns, 'Some rousing motions': the plurality of Miltonic ideology', *Literature and the English Civil War*, op. cit., pp. 110–26; see also Mary Anne Radzinowicz, *Towards Samson Agonistes: The Growth of Milton's Mind* (Princeton, Princeton University Press, 1978).
[2] W. R. Parker, *Milton: A Biography* (Oxford, Clarendon Press, 1968).
[3] Christopher Hill, *Milton and the English Revolution* (London, Faber, 1977).

ideas which scholars can trace back to antiquity were commonplaces to seventeenth-century radical groups such as the Levellers and Ranters. Milton gathered his ideas not only from older books but from contemporary pamphlets issued by those frequently characterised by the social and cultural elite – then as now – as being on the lunatic fringe. We have become aware that Milton's poetry as well as prose was designed to intervene in specific political instances, negotiating these through both elite and popular cultural resources. In such circumstances, even if the date of *Samson*'s composition remains problematised, attention shifts to the date of its first publication in 1671. The poem obviously engages with Milton's experience of the revolution's defeat following the Restoration, and, given Milton's well-known support for Commonwealth and Protectorate, it is difficult to imagine a reader in the early 1670s perceiving the poem as evolving out of the period of the late 1640s, a time which many supporters of the English Revolution experienced as one of hope and triumph. *Samson Agonistes*'s presentation of a hero whose refusal to capitulate allows him to regain divine inner light and inflict a defeat on his enemies bears witness to the plea for continued resistance of the type a republican supporter would propose during a time of defeat. Christopher Hill has emphasised how Milton explicitly has Samson bring down the temple on 'Lords, ladies, captains, counsellors, or priests,/Their choice nobility and flower' (11.1653–4) allowing the vulgar [i.e. the common people] 'who stood without' to escape.[1] Milton departs from the biblical account which has the people suffer with their rulers. This seems a clear example of his allegiance to popular dissent against the Church and social elite who supported the Restoration.

What it is important to recognise here is that a text's negotiation with the time of its historical production is a complex operation. With *Samson* we have to decide whether we should concentrate on the time of its circulation in the early 1670s or whether we should attempt to determine a precise date of composition. A text can take on a very different character through the circumstances of its

[1] Ibid, pp. 438–9.

But surely the universal message remains primary whatever the historical relevance.

circulation: when it finds publication, who publishes it, and what were the terms of its publication – for example, in a cheap edition offering wide access or an expensive limited edition intended for a specific audience. These issues will play a significant part in determining the circumstances of original reception. We need also to ask questions about why certain styles and generic forms were adopted at specific moments. A text's style as well as content signals social, cultural, political affinities and expectations. *Samson Agonistes* employs the prophetic use of Scripture beloved of the English radical tradition during the period.[1] Though set in a biblical past, the poem used the popular application of typology to indicate a present importance. Since history was commonly seen as a working out of scriptural promise, what had been figured forth in the Old Testament (the original story of Samson) was accomplished in the New Testament (by Christ as second Samson winning a more lasting victory) and repeated in succeeding times (the present conflict of the godly suffering under the yoke of royalist Philistines). The poem proposes that a cause which appeared to be defeated could be revived through God's agency. It seems to speak this most loudly to those supporters of Protestant prophecy and millennarianism, those who were, like the Ranters, among the most radical supporters of the revolution. The poem can be seen offering a political agenda through its expectation of a manner of reading Scripture, a manner most popular among those who viewed the Restoration as defeat.

This is only part of *Samson Agonistes'* contextualisation. Certainly, circulating in the world of the 1670s, the poem can be seen as important to groups of Protestant dissenters, offering them a visionary politics founded both on the scripturally based structure of history they favoured but also by appropriating and re-employing the scriptural Word which was a familiar practice of their own revolutionary writing. Yet, the style of *Samson* is fundamentally different from those texts associated with the writing of popular radical groups. Milton adopts a classical tragic high style

[1] For discussions of the relation between scriptural language and mid-seventeenth-century writing see N. H. Keeble, *The Literary Culture of Nonconformity in Later Seventeenth-Century England* (Leicester, Leicester University Press, 1987); Nigel Smith, *Perfection Proclaimed: Language and Literature in English Radical Religion 1640–1660* (Oxford, Clarendon Press, 1989), esp. pp. 229–348.

and models *Samson* to participate in Renaissance human-ist *parodia Christiana*, the transference of Classical literary principles to Christian settings, a methodology common throughout Europe from the fifteenth century onwards especially among neo-Latin writing. The poem stylistically asserts its participation in high literary culture, a culture by the 1670s unquestionably associated with a social elite. In contrast popular dissenting tracts frequently insist on a strong separate identity, suspicious of being seen as formally composed and keen to assert scriptural language as a key to asserting their own experience. Among groups who believed the structures and orders of the Church – both Roman and English – had, from antiquity, pol-luted the immediacy of the 'Everlasting Gospel', formal literary language and highly organised stylistic expres-sion were viewed with suspicion,[1] and were frequently seen as one more medium through which God's truth had been fouled. This provoked popular writing which deliberately employed the unusual and seemingly random combination of styles in a uncertain structural organisation. This feature of popular writing has commonly resulted in severe judgements among those literary critics who see stylistic control as a fundamental criterion to judging a text's accomplishment.

It is characteristic of Milton to wish his audience to see him as a writer familiar with highly regarded literary writing and able to employ it to more serious purpose than it had been previously. *Samson Agonistes* is not centred on Greek legend which was the staple of classical tragedy but, as Milton's age believed, on Christian truth, and on truths capable of being repeated in Milton's present. Milton's adoption of the high style here distances him from popular dissenting expression, instead giving him a voice (if not a message) more likely to be equated with, and find favour among, a sophisticated court culture. Milton preferred many aspects of the religious, and perhaps even social, programmes that the more radical groups which came to prominence during the Commonwealth favoured. It is apparent, though, that he was extremely uneasy about the cultural manifestations of such programmes. Milton, as

[1] See Smith, *A Collection of Ranter Writings*, op. cit., pp. 30–8.

Marvell, was concerned to show that the establishment of a godly republic in England could produce writing which participated in established literary culture, indeed surpass previous achievements.

Importantly, too, the use of a high style allowed Milton a voice he might not otherwise have achieved during the Restoration. Even ten years after the re-establishment of monarchy, those in power were not keen to see the Protectorate's most eloquent defender openly engage in the unmistakable political rhetoric of the tract and pamphlet. For a restored social elite, one which included many former supporters of Parliament, the remaining dissenters were 'A turbulent, seditious, and factious people' and their written style of self-presentation was further confirmation of their unruliness.[1] Adopting a style whose crafted formality is at the other extreme from those promoted by radical groups, Milton is not openly proclaiming his continued rebelliousness. Stylistically, *Samson* is distancing itself from the very audience it should inspire, but by doing so Milton is helping to avoid potential censorship and a silencing altogether.

Samson Agonistes exemplifies a problem which has stood at the centre of current inquiry into the negotiations a text has with an historical context. If Milton adopts a high style which allows him to voice opposition to Restoration politics, is that opposition not contained by this style, one perceived as normally expressing the values of the elite? Does this cause Milton's text to become compromised, its message rendered politically neutered? We can point to Milton being retained as an approved poet of high literary culture during the next century when other dissenting writing of Milton's age circulated among groups increasingly only at the margins of political life. Milton's high style allowed *Samson* to be read in a manner which reassured the very groups it can be argued the poem attacks. Milton's maintenance of the traditional Renaissance literary values of art, imitation, and exercise allowed him to be appropriated by a culturally elitist agenda indivisibly caught up with an elitist social and political agenda. The questions

---

[1] See Christopher Hill, *A Turbulent, Seditious, and Factious People: John Bunyan and His Church* (Oxford, Oxford University Press, 1988). The phrase is Bunyan's own and refers to how he and his church were regarded by 'respectable' society in 1662.

raised by literature's interaction with power, vested in the
control of institutions and those who control them, has
been the focus of recent debate about how texts circulate
in history and is crucial to the arguments voiced in the
New Historicism which will be considered in detail in
Chapter 4.

What I wish to indicate here is that a new emphasis on a
text's negotiation with history does not allow us to reduce
literary texts to the status of documents, writing which
only exemplifies the preoccupations of certain periods past
and present. Questions about what may be termed the
aesthetics of a text continue to be posed, even though the
aesthetic is no longer tied to a text's autonomous integrity.
One complication that we see raised with *Samson Agonistes*,
is that a text's success in fulfilling the conditions of its
chosen genre, in this case classical tragedy, may help to
render it unsuccessful in terms of the way it was originally
envisaged as intervening aethestically in its contemporary
history. In this instance, the employment of a high style
to ensure a dissenting voice continues to be heard results
in an easy official appropriation of *Samson Agonistes* by an
elite culture empowered by the poem's style to construct
a reading of the 'tragedy' of Samson, a reading which
reduces the poem to celebrate a unique legendary/literary
figure whose suffering is discussed in terms of a generalised human condition. Milton's style, enabling the text
to circulate in a politically charged climate, also works
to enforce the distinctions between serious and popular
writing, ironically helping to marginalise the writings of
the very groups whose political agendas he shared. The
aesthetic, and how we analyse it, is not separated from
the political, but circulates with it.

Is *Samson Agonistes*, therefore, an aesthetically satisfying
or dissatisfying text? Given the confusions rendered by its
apparent message and a stylistic structure which subverts
this message (or, at least, creates an audience primarily
among those for whom such a message is unwelcome),
can we talk of the poem as a successful work of art? The
answers will largely depend on our own perspectives on
the past and the present, the way in which we, too, employ
a political aesthetic.

The General Introduction to *The Pelican Guide to English*

Literature saw the book's role as helping readers respond 'to what is living and contemporary in literature':

> Not that one is offering literature as a substitute religion or as providing a philosophy for life. Its satisfactions are of their own kind, though they are satisfactions intimately bound up with the life of each individual reader, and therefore not without their bearing on his attitude to life.[1]

The role of literature here is seen as largely inert: passive moral formation and entertainment. The idea of literary writing participating in active political agendas, intervening in the collective life of a society, helping to mould social transformation is a largely foreign concept to traditional literary criticism. As we can see, though, new concerns with how writing interacts with history are causing us to abandon the idea of literary study as something caught up with the transcendental. Our new critical practice is showing that the questions we pose on Renaissance writing, which insist on the importance of contextualisation, reflect our own concerns with the function of language and value within society. As we come to discover and worry about our own lack of autonomy, we discover in the past a similar lack of autonomy but, importantly in the Renaissance, a body of writing which never believed it possessed the power of independent expression in the first place. Within Renaissance writing we can discover evidence which reveals that a text's recognition that it circulates within a powerful institutional context need not be capitulation to context, but its own powerful representation of that context. Powerful because within the text lies the potential for transformation, not the mere passive reflection of history but a reorganisation of it, suggesting that history might be otherwise, representing the possiblity of change. Literary representation enters a complex negotiation with history, a debate about 'things' (institutions, actions, events) and the words used to name them with an awareness that both the names and the things may be otherwise.

[1] Ford (ed.), *The Pelican Guide*, op. cit., pp. 7–8.

2
Words not Things

New alignments between literature and history are only one feature of theory's impact on readings of Renaissance texts. Contemporary literary theory has also questioned whether a relation between words and things is easily achieved, even possible. Many cultural historians have too readily appropriated literary writing as cultural documents, subduing the problems about what language actually represents which have been examined by other forms of theoretical inquiry, notably deconstruction. As Paul de Man has pointed out:

> Literature is fiction not because it somehow refuses to acknowledge 'reality', but because it is not *a priori* certain that language functions according to principles which are those, or which are *like* those, of the phenomenal world. It is therefore not *a priori* certain that literature is a reliable source of information about anything but its own language.[1]

De Man's scepticism is indicative of a new type of formalism in approaching texts, where information exterior to the text itself (such as author, or period, or indeed the text's subject) is ignored or dismissed as incidental. Critical activity becomes focused instead on the play of language. Deconstruction further works to demonstrate that the integrity of a text – its ability to articulate a controlled self-sufficient statement – is impossible. Language, as Jacques Derrida has forcefully argued, is a field of play.[2] Language does not simply stand as a signifier for some thing, an exact reference between a word and a thing. Rather language acts as a substitute for the thing, or in Derrida's formulation it acts as a supplement.[3] For Derrida,

[1] Paul de Man, 'The resistance to theory' in David Lodge (ed.) *Modern Criticism and Theory: A Reader* (London, Longman, 1988) p. 362.
[2] Jacques Derrida, *Writing and Difference*, Alan Bass (trans.) (London, Routledge and Kegan Paul, 1978), esp. pp. 278–93.
[3] Jacques Derrida, *Of Grammatology*, Gayatri Chakravorty Spivak (trans.) (Baltimore, Johns Hopkins University Press, 1976), pp. 141–64, 269–316.

language replaces the signified thing. Language still retains a referential function but it also adds something. Discursive practice is not applying simple correspondences between things and the language used to signify them. Language is always something more. It acts as a supplement to a lack, something missing, on the part of the signified thing. Language, by not replacing the signified thing at the supposed centre of the structure it has created, discredits the idea of there being a centre at all. Within a text, we can no longer imagine some signified object outside of language, determining the language used to signify it.

A discursive practice, therefore, also resists any attempt at offering a total description, a point where meaning can be contained or exhausted. Discursive practices are rather fields of play, capable of infinite substitutions. As Derrida makes clear, this lack of totality with language – something he sees as one of its inevitable qualities – occurs because, as a supplement, it reveals that there is always something missing from language. That absence is a centre, the signified thing which language has substituted for. The true presence of the signified thing would arrest and limit the play of substitutions for it which language generates. But such a state is impossible. By questioning the idea of language as a total representation of what it signifies, deconstruction refuses to limit the play of language, refuses to acknowledge that it is controlled by a centre – an author, a historic identity, the subject which it is representing. By acting as a substitute, a supplement, to its ostensible signified, language is always suggesting the signified is somehow other than it appears in its linguistic signifying form. Deconstruction has been especially interested in exploring language as a supplement which de-centres the apparent organisation of the signified thing, revealing self-contradiction and instability.

In many respects deconstruction has not been avidly employed in analysing Renaissance texts and there is a certain contradiction in employing it in this study. By talking about Renaissance texts, or more accurately texts produced during a period defined by current readers as the Renaissance, we are attempting to provide a type of structure (how language operated in a defined period) which deconstruction, in some purist sense, would argue is to miss the point of how language acts as a supplement. In dealing with the Renaissance, we are assuming, as de Man above indicates, that there is a relation between language and the phenomenal (i.e. the range of activities undertaken in a defined historical period) which is an *a priori* given. This relationship may in fact be the result of convention, the very type of convention deconstructive criticism wishes to demystify.

Scepticism about the relation between words and things indeed raises a question about whether the Renaissance is a phenomenon or whether it is a signifier, a discursive practice, which acts as a supplement for, say, the activities of the early modern period which are the things ostensibly being signified by the term Renaissance. Under the terms of deconstruction, by proposing the Renaissance as a signifier, it suggests a lack, an absence in some sense, of 'Renaissance' from the early modern period. The Renaissance then can be seen as an addition to the early modern period. It becomes a term whose reference is linguistic and whose meaning is not determined by the phenomenon of the early modern period. The Renaissance becomes a field of play, a field where there are any possible number of substitutions to describe what it is. A field, further, where what would restrict what the Renaissance could be – the firm phenomenal centre of the early modern period – is missing. The Renaissance is not the early modern period, it is an additional something more and by breaking the equation, Renaissance = early modern, the Renaissance is no longer a stable controllable thing.

The point is an important one because, as de Man goes on to argue, what we call ideology is precisely the confusion of linguistic with natural reality or reference with phenomenalism.[1] As we have witnessed in the preceding chapter, the ideological contest for control of the past is largely predicated on the basis of the Renaissance being a phenomenon, something that can be discovered and controlled by accurate descriptions of what it is. The Renaissance is frequently presented as what is truest, best, and most pleasing about the early modern period. The actual phenomenon these qualitative attributes refer to is, as we

[1] de Man, op. cit., p. 363.

have witnessed, contested. But the assumption made by both historicist critical right and left is that the Renaissance does refer to something which can, potentially, be identified in a contained fashion. To satisfy the demands of their historicist ideologies it is necessary to promote Renaissance as a phenomenon, not a linguistic term whose field of reference is unstable and above all open. Yet, it is clear that our criticism must be aware of the supplemental aspect of the Renaissance – that it is not automatically a *something* open to contained description. As any term, Renaissance is not something fixed.

If deconstruction in a purest sense is only of limited interest to a study which is asserting that texts emerge out of a particular culture called the English Renaissance, it is also true that, fortunately, there is little pure deconstruction about. Derrida himself is interested in the tension created between discursive play and history. But new questions about the relations of language and what language represents are of great importance to our understanding of Renaissance culture. Certainly, similar questions were posed in the Renaissance and given that the study of language, particularly rhetoric, lay at the heart of humanist education programmes during the period this is not surprising. The equation of a person's worth, both morally and socially, with their ability to be eloquent is found iterated both implicitly and explicitly throughout the period. Sir Philip Sidney's argument in *The Defence of Poetry* that poetry's didactic superiority rested in its ability to both teach and delight is an example of a belief in the superiority of eloquent as opposed to plain language as the vehicle for communicating serious issues. Sidney's proposal that a poet's creation of pleasing fictions is a means of transcending nature and reaching toward an imitation of the divine is perceived as a means by which an experience of the world lost by original sin may be recaptured. Milton's *Of Education* expands Sidney's remarks on poetry to learning in general: 'The end, then, of Learning is, to repair the ruins of our first parents by regaining to know God aright' (p. 557). Within a humanist perception of language, therefore, was the ability to extend and supplement existing reality and to indicate a higher reality in a perfection phenomenally lost. This is not, in its own right, a Renaissance deconstructionist assertion about the absence of a signified. As Milton's own language above reveals learning 're-pairs', it re-establishes the link between us and a higher reality. The language signifier is perceived as potentially representing a lost signified. But by asserting the ability of language to create true fictions, this celebration of the power of language is also helping to de-centre language's supposed referential relation with the world of epistemological things.

In claiming one of the qualities of language was its ability to supplement the phenomenal reality of this world, the Renaissance also acknowledged the volatility of language. Language might be able to illuminate higher 'things', but an admission of its fictive role also made it suspect. This was particularly true of the highly organised rhetoric of some literary language. George Puttenham's *Arte of English Poesy*, for example, readily acknowledges that rhetorical figures can 'abuse' a relation between words and things by creating a doubleness. This doubleness is not dissimilar to a deconstructive view of language as a field of play:

> As figures be the instruments of ornament in euery lan-
> guage, so be they also in a sorte abuses or rather trespasses
> in speach, because they passe the ordinary limits of com-
> mon vtterance, and be occupied of purpose to deceiue the
> eare and also the minde, drawing it from plainnesse and
> simplicitie to a certaine doublenesse whereby our talke is
> the more guilefull & abusing.[1]

As Derek Attridge has demonstrated, Puttenham is forced to rely on the idea of decorum to argue that poets can transform the 'vices' of rhetoric to virtues in their use of art to perfect rather than pervert nature.[2] Decorum, though, is not readily definable for Puttenham. It remains an (unac-knowledged) slippery circular concept for him. Decorum, Puttenham proposed, is a quality which comes naturally to the elite, but these elite are identified by their natural sense of decorum. As Attridge shows this means that poetry claiming to be perfecting the natural (acting according to

[1] George Puttenham, *The Arte of English Poesie*, The Third Booke of Ornament, ch. VII, 'Of Figures and Figurative Speaches', in G. Gregory Smith (ed.) *Elizabethan Critical Essays*, vol.2 (London, Oxford University Press, 1904), pp. 159–60.
[2] Derek Attridge, 'Puttenham's Perplexity: Nature, Art, and the Supplement in Renaissance Poetic Theory', in Patricia Parker and David Quint (eds) *Literary Theory/Renaissance Texts* (Baltimore, Johns Hopkins University Press, 1986), pp. 257–79.

decorum) establishes its claim to do so by using a rhetoric which is employed only by a learned few whose language is distanced from the natural language of the majority. What has formally been thought of as natural is marginalised as rude and barbarous. What is now considered natural is the result of learned artifice. For Attridge, Puttenham truly supplements nature with art, by substituting art for nature. Art occupies the centre from which nature is now absent.

It is noticeable how Renaissance theorists of literature elide the problem of language being employed in deceitful ways to create self-contradictory and unstable assertions. Most, of course, had a vested interest in promoting eloquence as a means by which civilised, moral, and socially superior behaviour could be recognised. Sidney's *Defence of Poetry* for instance assumes a hostile critical environment, maintaining that there are important groups who mistrust poetic fictions altogether. Sidney as a poet, therefore, understandably asserts the improving role of poetry against those hostile to literature. Scepticism about literary language, however, was not only the province of those opposed in some absolutist sense to literary practices. Language's power to deceive, misdirect and generally subvert literary practice while supposedly promoting 'truth' is a feature exploited by many literary practiioners within their own writing.

Consider Sidney's first sonnet of his sequence *Astrophil and Stella*:

> Loving in truth, and fain in verse my love to show,
> That she (dear she) might take some pleasure of my pain;
> Pleasure might cause her read, reading might make her know;
> Knowledge might pity win, and pity grace obtain;
>   I sought fit words to paint the blackest face of woe,
> Studying inventions fine, her wits to entertain;
> Oft turning others' leaves, to see if thence would flow
> Some fresh and fruitful showers upon my sunburnt brain.
>   But words came halting forth, wanting inventions's stay;
> Invention, nature's child, fled step-dame study's blows;
> And others' feet still seemed but strangers in my way.
> Thus great with child to speak, and helpless in my throes,
>   Biting my truant pen, beating myself for spite,
>   'Fool', said my muse to me; 'look in thy heart, and write.'[1]

[1] Katherine Duncan-Jones (ed.), *Sir Philip Sidney: Selected Poems* (Oxford, Clarendon Press, 1973), p. 117.

The opening assertion 'Loving in truth, and fain in verse my love to show' signals a confusion. Does Astrophil, who is the ostensible author, mean he loves truth or that it is true he is in love? He is disposed to show his love, or his love of truth, in verse, but 'fain' also acknowledges a (at least potential) feigning of this condition in verse. A feigning could indicate that the poet is actually interested in creating a false portrayal of his love. The line can be read: It is true that I am in love and wish to reveal this love in poetry. Or it could mean, I am in love and will present this love in such a way as to win advantage (the next lines make clear Astrophil's wish to obtain Stella's 'grace' (both spiritual blessing and sexual favours). Other combinations are also possible: e.g. 'I prefer truth but also wish to represent my love in verse.' This last interpretation might confirm Astrophil as a lover of truth through his acknowledgement that a representation of love in verse is artificial, that he is feigning. Or the line could be denying that there is any contradiction at all between truth and feigning (poetry, Sidney claimed in his *Defence*, could make true fictions). There are a vast number of potential meanings made possible by the volatility of language. A volatility emphasised by the juxtaposition of truth and showing and the pun on 'fein'. Only by supplying something outside the poem – claims for intention, the ostensible participation of the language in recognisable (and thus containable) poetic conventions, the equation of Astrophil with Sidney and his love with Penelope Rich (the sequence's Stella) and then a testing of the language's claim against their history – could the referential quality of the poem's language be critically maintained. Such impositions on the poem are almost invariably imposed in critical accounts but, as we see, the play of the language resists such containments. Linguistically, the line acknowledges that the representation of Astrophil's love – and what or who is not clear, Stella or his own self-absorption – may be feigned, a false and therefore different presentation of his love. The relation between verse and what it apparently seeks to signify is disrupted and made unstable. The poetry substitutes for the love and for the lovers – Astrophel's and Stella's reality is also only within the bounds of linguistic play.

Sidney's sonnet concludes with the injunction. ' "Fool",

said my muse to me; "look in thy heart, and write".'
The muse's intervention occurs after Astrophil appears
to be carried away in a violent frenzy, unable to find a
fit language to achieve his ends. Of course, the disorgan-
ised pattern to Astrophil's argument is wholly contrived.
This discourse is formed within a closely structured sonnet, and the muse's intervention is a conclusion which
maintains the sonnet's structure. Once more, though, the
poem reveals a play of language which render meaning
unstable and even self-contradictory. The muse is a poetic
convention and its appearance here to demand the authenticity of Astrophil's feelings (look in thy heart) is ironic.
But the muse's intervention also raises the possibility of
abandoning poetry altogether. Writing from the heart is
the recommendation of a muse who could be seeking to
make such writing a legitimate part of poetry, an activity
which takes place under the muse's control. But it could
also signify that writing from the heart is different from
poetry, the muse's injunction being meant as a dismissal,
exiling Astrophil from poetry's realm. The compatibility
between poetry and writing from the heart is not auto-
matic but at best conventional. Indeed, within Renaissance
convention, the two do not have the clear associations they
do within Romantic conventions. Poetry, as Sidney argued
in the *Defence*, is art, imitation, and exercise. Astrophil
has been trying in the sonnet to proceed by imitation
and been singularly unsuccessful in doing so. The muse's
outburst may be interpreted as an exasperated sentence
of banishment. Astrophil is a fool incapable of writing
poetry.

   The sonnets of *Astrophil and Stella* that follow may be the
result of taking the muses' advice or ignoring the advice.
The sonnets may announce a compatibility between poetic
convention and authentic expression; or the sonnets may
be the result of Astrophil staying within the muse's
domain, writing in imitation of familiar poetic norms and
abandoning the muse's advice to look for an authentic
writing from the heart. The next sonnet in the sequence
begins with Astrophil looking at his heart and finding
there the conventional poetic image of love's wounding
arrow. The sonnet concludes with him employing all his
wit to make his love appear differently from what his

experience tells him it is. There are other meanings to be drawn from this first sonnet, of course, but what is clear is that the poetic sequence of *Astrophil and Stella* may be seen announcing itself as a failure, a success, both, or neither. The sonnet's language allows a continuous play of substitutions. Its meaning only becomes contained when exterior intentions are imposed – insisting that it operates according to Petrarchan or anti-Petrarchan convention, that the sonnet's explore the relation between sexual behaviour at court and ritual descriptions of this behaviour, that the sequence is a concealed articulation of Sidney's relation with Penelope Rich. In each case linguistic play will be restricted by reference to something the language may not refer to at all. The sonnet registers forcibly its linguistic uncertainty, rendering its own meaning unstable, and interestingly also de-centring the external conventions which attempt to contain it.

Another good example of Renaissance poetry's attempt to explore the relation between signifying language and signified thing is offered by Shakespeare's sonnet 54:

O, how much more doth beauty beauteous seem
By that sweet ornament which truth doth give!
The rose looks fair, but fairer we it deem
For that sweet odour which doth in it live.
The canker-blooms have full as deep a dye
As the perfumed tincture of the roses,
Hang on such thorns, and play as wantonly
When summer's breath their masked buds discloses;
But for their virtue only is their show,
They lived unwoo'd, and unrespected fade;
Die to themselves. Sweet roses do not so;
Of their sweet deaths are sweetest odours made.
And so of you, beauteous and lovely youth,
When that shall vade, by verse distills your truth.

Here the conventional representation of truth as the unadorned, stable centre which poetic ornamentation covers is replaced by a claim that truth is an ornament, an addition which paradoxically makes beauty *seem* more beautiful. Truth becomes a supplement to a thing, in the analogy of the rose, it becomes the rose's scent. But despite being a supplement it also replaces what it signifies. The addition of scent to a rose is the way we recognise it as a true rose. The addition of ornament to beauty makes beauty truly appear beauteous. Using this analogy, the sonnet looks to gain power over a youth's beauty by arguing that showy flowers merely fade but true scented roses in their death are distilled into perfume which become, paradoxically, their sweetest moment as roses:

> And so of youth, beauteous and lovely youth,
> When that shall vade, by verse distills your truth.

A recognisable conventional poetic strategy of indicating the power of verse to create lasting reputation, with the usual implication that what the poet actually desires is physical enjoyment of the transitory beauty, is here rendered unstable. The truth of the youth's beauty will be distilled by the addition of poetic ornament which makes it seem more beautiful. The truth of the object is immaterial, what the sonnet argues is that truth is created by distilling (transforming) the youth's beauty into poetry. To achieve this 'youth' must first fade away. On the rose analogy there must in fact be violence done to beauty, it must certainly be destroyed before beauty can be made truly beautiful by the addition of scent or verse in their most powerful concentrated forms as perfume or sonnet.

To capture the truth of the object then, the poem argues, the object must be absent. Or at least seem to be absent. For what the sonnet also reveals is that the truth of verse is not only ornamental addition, it is all there is. The faded youth only exists within the realm of the poem, his or her traces have otherwise vanished, necessarily so to make the verses' truth actually true. The creation of poetic truth is achieved only through the destruction of what it seeks to represent. Rather than creating a permanent signifier of the youth's beauty, the sonnet seeks the destruction of the beauty and its replacement by a beauty supplied by verse. This additional beauty becomes the true and only beauty of the absent youth. But it is a beauty without subject, a field of discursive play capable of infinitely ornamenting with 'truth' what it has destroyed and replaced.

Within the terms the sonnet has constructed, any claim to truth, even poetic truth, is necessarily compromised and made self-contradictory. Truth becomes a supplement, a substitute which replaces something which is missing.

Claiming to possess within the sonnet's language the truth of the youth's beauty is now to admit an absent centre. This truth no longer points to a signified. The poem which is addressed to a youth is claiming the absence of that youth, necessarily destroyed by the verse which has distilled his faded beauty's 'truth'. The sonnet has not given the youth a new centre, a pretty room, within the poem. By claiming truth as an ornament, the sonnet insists that the youth's truth must also be supplemental to the sonnet, different from it. The sonnet which apparently seeks to contain the truth of the youth's beauty so as to gain power and control over it, exposes that it destroys and banishes the youth's beauty. What remains is only language, the sonnet. But it is a language once again demonstrated to be volatile, unable to have its discursive play controlled, de-centring any attempt at a structured organisation.

Derrida's recognition of a tension created between the play of language and history has been matched in recent years by an attempt by some critics to force a polarisation between critical activities which embrace history from those which embrace linguistic theory.[1] In fact, though, most influential work on Renaissance texts has recognised a place for both history and analysis alert to the shifts and instabilities of language in explorations of texts. If there is little unfettered deconstructive activity operating within Renaissance studies currently, it is largely because the questions critics wish to ask of texts are premised on ideas opposed to accepting that a text cannot speak about anything but itself. Literary studies are increasingly directed towards cultural studies, of understanding the way texts operate with social structures. Similarly, during the Renaissance, humanist theory was directed at language in action. Its preoccupations with rhetoric and oratory envisaged public forms where language was used to persuade, exhort, or otherwise move. Literary language was not removed from these public concerns, a belief that texts could communicate and move readers was of course fundamental to the assumption that poetry could teach and delight. It is, perhaps not surprising that Renaissance

---

[1] See J. Hillis Miller, 'Presidential Address 1986, the triumph of theory, the resistance to reading and the question of the material base', op. cit. (see Preface, p. 5, note 1).

writers seem most open to the deconstructive implications of the play of language in lyric poetry, generic forms which suggest more personal and private preoccupations. Some of the common strategies deployed within lyrics, for instance creating the impression of the lyric's reader as an intruder gazing voyeuristically into texts meant for private circulation, is one of the devices employed by poets to protect themselves. Such devices are ways of deflecting accusations that the linguistic instability their poems expose might be read as undermining public discourses which are anxious to maintain the semblance of the relation between word and thing in, for example, celebratory accounts of influential court figures.[1] The text's instabilities, this device suggests, are the result of the reader straying into private discourses, where the terms of reference are apparently explicit to the knowing 'other' reader, the person addressed who is ostensibly real but in actuality normally a fictional construction.

An awareness of the volatility of language, among Renaissance writers and among current critics, has proved extremely valuable in drawing attention to clashes, inconsistency, and points of confrontation within texts. It has led to our recognition of the difficulties inherent in the codes which texts employ to articulate what could otherwise not have been written, of the difficult negotiations between ideological expression and the things this expression seeks to characterise and thus control, and of the complexities of a text's own negotiations with other texts. Importantly, by enabling us to see the lack of stability within textual play, deconstruction has helped bring attention to the exterior forces which attempt to control such play. Recent criticism has become increasingly interested in the institutions which seek to impose controls on what we can say about the Renaissance. As we have seen in the preceding chapter, some of these controls have overtly political agendas.

[1] See David Javitch, *Poetry and Courtliness in Renaissance England* (Princeton, Princeton University Press, 1978); for specific location of Sidney's sequence see Ann Rosalind Jones and Peter Stallybrass, 'Courtship and courtiership: the politics of Astophil and Stella' *Studies in English Literature*, 24, (1984), 53–68; Clark Hulse, 'Stella's Wit: Penelope Rich as Reader of Sidney's Sonnets', in Margaret W. Ferguson, Maureen Quilligan and Nancy J. Vickers (eds) *Rewriting the Renaissance: The Discourses of Sexual Difference in Early Modern Europe*, (Chicago, University of Chicago Press, 1986), pp. 272–86.

In others, the political becomes subtly incorporated into other forms of institutional control. What we read is commonly determined for us. Our experience as readers is formed, in part, from the texts we are given to read.

3
Founding Canons

Many teachers believe that Shakespeare's work conveys universal values, and that his language expresses rich and subtle meanings beyond that of any other English writer. Other teachers point out that evaluations of Shakespeare have varied from one historical period to the next, and they argue that pupils should be encouraged to think critically about his status in the canon. But almost everyone agrees that his work should be represented in a National Curriculum. Shakespeare's plays are so rich that in every age they can produce fresh meanings and even those who deny his universality agree on his cultural importance.

This extract from *English for ages 5 to 16: Proposals of the Secretary of State for Education and Science* published by the British government in 1989 as a consultative paper for the planned National Curriculum in England and Wales is an appropriate place to begin a consideration of the institutional framework in which we study Renaissance literature. The *Proposals* were to advise government on appropriate 'attainment targets and programmes of study for English' that students might be expected to gain (in the case of thia extract) at secondary schools. The critical suppositions behind the study of Shakespeare, as we can see, are largely traditionalist with some recognition of a new emphasis on cultural studies. There appears to be an air of condescension towards those who refuse to recognise Shakespeare's universality, as though they were a peculiar sect within the broad church of liberalism. What is clear, though, is that Shakespeare's presence on the National Curriculum is to represent both a timeless cultural importance and one specific to the Renaissance.

A select number of Shakespeare's plays have become the only sustained acquaintance with Renaissance literature a majority of readers are likely to have before entering higher education. Despite the stated belief in the *Proposals* that students at school should be exposed to a historic range of English writing, there is little attention to works written before the nineteenth century, and certainly no recognition that new relations with history are causing literary texts to be approached in new ways. Shakespeare is re-allocated the central place in the canon. We all agree on the cultural importance of Shakespeare, the Report asserts, and we probably all do. What is not voiced is that this importance is, in part at least, caused by the institutional processes which give Shakespeare a privileged position on the curriculum at schools. What is implied, rather, is that Shakespeare's cultural importance is somehow intrinsic and not the product of powerful formative institutions such as school boards.

I am not trying to suggest that there is some conspiracy at work to centralise the importance of Shakespeare when it should be more widely shared or go to some other figure. There is enormous value in having a body of Renaissance texts which we can assume a large number of readers have some acquaintance with. Shakespeare's centrality has been achieved because there remains continued debate about the plays, these texts do not come down to us as 'dead on arrival', to borrow a phrase from Stephen Greenblatt.[1] But it is varying cultural transactions of the past which encouraged Shakespeare's plays to remain in wide circulating which empower Shakespeare's continued circulation. The plays become a focus, not only for question about Renaissance drama, but about a variety of cultural debates. 'Shakespeare' has become more than a collection of Renaissance texts and is now a site for wider cultural explorations and controversies. For example, a Sunday newspaper recently carried a column entitled 'A Book that Changed Me' in which the playwright David Edgar extolled George Steiner's *The Death of Tragedy*, a book he was introduced to by a programme note for a production of *King Lear*. Edgar noted how the Royal Shakespeare Company's programmes 'were a treasure house of enticing quotations that led the keen reader on to find and study the books themselves'.[2] The critical value of Shakespeare is not founded only in the texts ascribed to him, but in wider circulations and negotiations of Shakespeare within social

[1] Stephen Greenblatt, *Shakespearean Negotiations* (Oxford, Clarendon Press, 1988), p. 7.
[2] *The Independent on Sunday*, 1 April, 1990.

frameworks, in the moment of his texts' original production and in subsequent periods. A text's value rests partly
then on the demand for it, and that demand is predicated
on previous demand. Shakespeare's high valuation is supported by institutions who ensure his texts are read, these
accumulated acts of reading forming part of the value
placed on a widely negotiable Shakespearean currency.

One of the difficulties confronting students of Renaissance literature is that, at a time when critical and cultural theory is asking us to expand our familiarity with
a wider range of reading, it is increasingly difficult to
have access to the range of texts we would like to read.
Shakespeare is given a special status. In Britain there is a
large and welcome constituency for courses which study
his writing. The plays' prominence with the public are
assured because of a Shakespeare industry operating
in theatres, in tourist boards, and because of the centrality of his work with school examining boards. This
industry should certainly not be haughtily condescended
to. It allows an audience whose access to Renaissance
writing would otherwise be non-existent to gain some
insight into the past and witness some of the power of
its expression. An assured interest in Shakespeare supports the availability of a large number of editions of the
plays from cheap *Complete Works* to the specialist Arden
editions (still relatively affordable). It is a different story
with virtually every other writer.

In his *Elizabethan World Picture* Tillyard proposed the
book's purpose as 'to help the ordinary reader to understand and to enjoy the great writers of the age'.[1] The
constituency that made up these ordinary readers was
probably no more ordinary than Tillyard's projected
Elizabethans were, yet his assumption was of a body
of readers outside higher education institutions. Tillyard
could defend his belief in such a body by the existence
of a considerable number of Renaissance texts in cheap,
modern editions which general readers had access to.
This body of texts has largely disappeared. Renaissance
texts in circulation today are effectively course texts
designed, produced, and circulated among students in

---

[1] Tillyard, op. cit., p. 8 (see Chapter 1, note 1).

higher education or among a very small academic elite who make use of institutional libraries.

In certain respects the current conditions of the availability of texts create an increasing downward spiral about what types of material can be easily studied. Texts are selected for courses from among those available. The idea of mounting a course, say, in English Civil War poetry is fraught with an endless succession of practical difficulties because selections of poets such as Lovelace, Cowley, Wither, Thomas May, Thomas Stanley and so forth are not available. The easier option is to settle for looking at Milton and Marvell and a few lyrics by Henry Vaughan. The result of this process of 'making do' with what is available is that any likelihood of collections of such presently unavailable poets appearing are rendered even more economically impossible. Instead academic publishers compete in duplication the same market, publishing different editions of the same small selection of writing. Publishers will not publish chancy, fat collections when they can publish a small number of readily marketable volumes. For example, a number of academics waited with great interest for the Virago Press book, *Kissing the Rod: An Anthology of Seventeenth-century Women's Verse* (1988).[1] Pre-publication, it was announced in both hard and paperback format, the latter priced so that the book could be used as a course book. But when the volume was first published it appeared only as an expensive hardback and the opportunity for exploring an important range of writing was restricted to specialists and students willing to pass around a library copy. In late 1990 a paperback appeared but priced at double the cost in the pre-publication announcement, placing the volume outside the price range for a course text. The publisher had made a decision, no doubt on sound commercial information, about the viability of the book as a course text and decided it should have a more restricted clientele who are in a position to buy a large-format, expensive paperback.

One of the features of Ben Jonson's *Workes 1616* was not only that Jonson was the first English dramatist to present his plays as worthy of serious literary attention but also

[1] Germaine Greer, Susan Hastings, Jeslyn Medoff, Melinda Sansone (eds) *Kissing the Rod: An Anthology of Seventeenth Century Women's Verse* (London, Virago, 1988).

that he did so in a folio format. The size and consequent high cost of the book made Jonson's audience necessarily restricted to certain classes of readers. As his Latin epitaph on the title page announced, Jonson *Workes* were for the select few, not only serious readers but also affluent and socially well-positioned readers. The economics of the book trade today are creating conditions where many important texts are not only beyond purchase by students but by salaried staff as well. Only institutions, under increasing restrictions, can buy many important editions. The result is that the unit price becomes even higher as publishers protect their desired profit margin. Even more worrying, important academic publishers are commissioning fewer and fewer editions of Renaissance texts outside an increasingly narrow canon.

What is studied is substantially determined by what is available to study. One of the factors which helps form literary canons are the economics of the book market and the way institutions consequently react in constructing courses. It may be that the growth of desk-top publishing will allow a wider circulation of material (a great advantage of Renaissance texts is that they present few copyright problems), but there is little evidence so far. I have previously outlined the possibilities of political constraints on what we study. We can now add economic constraints. We must further admit institutional constraints in the form of the time available to study Renaissance writing on a degree course. All of these factors, some of which probably appear very mundane to readers waiting to tangle with texts and theory, contribute to the formation of literary canons. A canon may not be a bad thing in itself, but within the institution it is worthwhile for both staff and students to ask why we are studying these texts? What types of representative status do they possess? How are they culturally empowered? Institutional factors are one further area for which our critical practice needs to account.

There is no doubt that our experience of reading is involved with our previous reading experiences. We compare and contrast such experiences, constructing a sense of a text through its intertextual relations with other texts with which we are already familiar. It is noticeable how the novel has become the literary form on which discussions of texts in other generic forms are based. Thus, we will frequently think of character or characterisation in drama or poetry in terms of novels, and particularly the novels which stress psychological interiority. Discussions of plays, for instance, can often be seen to be founded on the unde-clared assumption that a dramatic figure represents a self (rather than a vehicle for dramatic ideas). The soliloquy in Renaissance texts is frequently given a special prominence because readers (and the assumption is of play readers rather than audiences witnessing a production) believe they are experiencing a moment of privileged revelation where the dramatist reveals a character's interiority. Take the following example from *Julius Caesar* where Brutus ostensibly debates the ground for killing Caesar:

> It must be by his death; and for my part,
> I know no personal cause to spurn at him,
> But for the general: he would be crown'd.
> How that might change his nature, there's the question.
> It is the bright day that brings forth the adder,
> And that craves wary walking. Crown him – that!
> And then, I grant, we put a sting in him
> That at his will he may do danger with.
> Th' abuse of greatness is when it disjoins
> Remorse from power; and to speak truth of Caesar,
> I have not known when his affections sway'd
> More than his reason. But 'tis a common proof
> That lowliness is young ambition's ladder,
> Whereto the climber-upward turns his face;
> But when he once attains the upmost round,
> He then unto the ladder turns his back,
> Looks in the cloud, scorning the base degrees
> By which he did ascend. So Caesar may.
> Then, lest he may, prevent. And since the quarrel
> Will bear no colour for the thing he is,
> Fashion it thus – that what he is, augmented,
> Would run to these and these extremities;
> And therefore think him as a serpent's egg,
> Which, hatch'd would as his kind grow mischievous,
> And kill him in the shell.
>
> (II, i, 10–34)

This is commonly perceived as a interior debate as Brutus tries to decide what should be done. But it hardly seems a dramatic articulation of character. As the language with

its repeated serpent imagery suggests, the speech is concerned with finding a public representation of the grounds
for killing Caesar. Brutus is certain of what he intends as the
speech opens: 'It must be by his death.' What he is concerned
with is the discovery of the right formulation to 'fashion
it thus', a means of presentation that will persuade an
audience that Caesar needed to die and was killed by
actions undertaken in the public rather than in a private
interest. What Caesar is will have to be re-presented by
Brutus: 'since the quarrel will bear no colour for the thing he
is'. Brutus's choice of Caesar as the serpent's egg is selected
as the suitable formulation of the equation between Caesar
and serpents Brutus has been toying with throughout. The
speech is a good example of formal rhetorical argument
by analogy rather than logic. It shows Brutus adept in the
use of rhetoric and looking forward to his public defence
of Caesar's assassination to the Roman crowd. The speech
does not create a distance between the public arguments
used and the imagined private moments. Brutus's self is
one founded on his public and not his private identity.
Brutus and the other characters can be presented as rep-
resentatives of political actions: the play explores the lack
of distance between private and public relations. All the
characters are fashioning actions through words, so that
the quality of both words and actions become unsettled,
dependent on political expediency.

Aristotle claimed that tragedy was the imitation of an
action and that character was an important but supplemen-
tary consideration.[1] Characters enacted the drama, but
tragedy was principally concerned with the actions which
resulted. The Renaissance inherited the symbolic moral
dramas of the Middle ages and, while Renaissance drama
devoted an increased importance to the complexitites of
the agents who enact the drama, it does not automatically
follow that the plays' central preoccupations are with character.[2]

Concentration on character may be argued to allow critical misconstruction about how the plays' dramatic action

[1] Aristotle, *The Poetics in Aristotle Horace Longinus: Classical Literary Criticism*, T. S. Dorsch (tran.) (Harmondsworth, Penguin, 1965) p. 39.
[2] See Catherine Belsey, *The Subject of Tragedy: Identity and Difference in Renaissance Drama* (London, Methuen, 1985).

works. The proposal that drama somehow became more sophisticated with an interest in psychology adopted by Shakespeare and Jacobean dramatists is to come to Renaissance drama with a presumption that literary sophistication is the representation of psychological interiority, a view largely derived from the centrality of late nineteenth and early twentieth century novels within a reading experience. It does not diminish *Julius Caesar* or make it less complex to approach it as a dramatised representation of the relation between words and actions within politics.

What *Julius Caesar*, and Renaissance drama generally, requires is a rethinking of how characters work as representations, a challenge to find a critical language which enables us to rethink the relation between symbol and character in a sophisticated way. To do so it is necessary to examine the origins of our literary expectations which so frequently assume that the best literary experience deals with individuals capable of making moral distinctions and to question the pejorative critical formulations which tend to accompany assessments of characters as vehicles for ideas: caricature, static, incompletely realised, and so on. Within *Julius Caesar* Antony's claim at the play's conclusion that 'this was the noblest Roman of them all' is frequently taken as some type of authentic commentary on Brutus and becomes the focus for critical exploration into Brutus's character. Nobility is taken as self-defined, a virtue which right-thinking readers ought to recognise, or a Roman ideal the terms of which the play defines (and sympathises with). But the play may be seen to represent 'Roman nobility' as a highly questionable ideal, a manner of staging oneself within a realm of political theatre. 'Nobility' is not an intrinsic quality, but a publicly defined attribute supported by birth and education (the conspirators and Antony, the play suggests, all went to school together – I, ii, 294–5). What Brutus or any of the characters 'really are' is not the centre of their dramatic interest. The play's interest, rather, is centred on how they act: both what they do and what they say, and the gap between the two.

Institutions form canons and work to maintain hierarchies within them. It is interesting to note with *Julius Caesar* the way scholarship has tried to support a reading of the play that promotes Brutus's statements as authentic revelations of his character. By believing the play explores a supposedly innate moral virtue such as nobility, the tragedy can be one focused on the interiority of the character and thus, so the assumption proceeds, it may be considered 'great'. Since the play is by Shakespeare, the critical policy has been to assume the tragedy must be of the first stature and, therefore, the play would be written to support this revelation of interiority. Ostensibly objective textual scholarship adopted editorial policies which for many years worked to ensure the above assumptions could be confirmed. The most notorious example in *Julius Caesar* was the scenes where Brutus reacts to the death of his wife Portia. The problem appeared because Brutus tells Cassius of Portia's death (and uses it to explain his bad temper towards Cassius). Brutus then, a few lines later, claims no knowledge of her death when two of his officers tell him of it (IV, iii, 141–92). Editors invented elaborate textual corruptions to explain this, claiming for instance that Shakespeare had written two different versions of Brutus's reactions and that the text used for the 1623 Folio (where the play first appeared) had mistakenly copied them both.[1] The design was apparently to leave readers with the impression that Brutus was genuinely applying stoical philosophy to contain the shock of losing Portia.

The actions of editorial emendation in this instance worked to suppress the scene's representation of Brutus as a role player. As Cassius remarks when Brutus has impressed the officers of his stoical resolve in accepting Portia's death: 'I have as much of this in art as you,/But yet my nature could not bear it so' (IV, iii, 192–3). Cassius is interested, too, in role-playing but is less successful at it than Brutus. The scene does not necessarily present Brutus in an unfavourable light. His collected resolve in front of his officers is assuring his troops' confidence in his controlled capacity to lead them as they prepare for an impending battle. His action as a general is sensible. But what was clear is that editors, believing that the play was about the intrinsically moral Brutus, could not accept a feigning Brutus and so explained away, or repressed, the scene where that role playing is most

[1] See for example, T. S. Dorsch (ed.) *Julius Caesar*, The Arden Shakespeare (London, Methuen, 1955) pp. 106–7.

formally represented. Believing that tragic greatness was founded on an exploration of a great individual, the literary institution found ways of assuring that Shakespeare's plays observed their premises. What could not be allowed was the suggestion that major characters were using language to deceive and self-present in expedient ways which suited political needs rather than the way they 'really were'.[1]

Literary canons, therefore, are arranged to support the (usually) unvoiced assumptions upon which study of them is founded. By articulating and then exploring these assumptions we discover the cultural and institutional process which has helped to create and sustain these canons. In questioning the theoretical position on which canons are grounded the possibility of other contending critical discourses with focuses outside canonical groupings become increasingly possible. One of the most powerful forms of inquiry in recent years has been to look at Renaissance writing produced outside the cultural elite, bringing attention to texts marginalised and ignored by the institutional processes which maintains the traditional canon.

Sir Philip Sidney's claim in *The Defence of Poetry* that poetry was the consequence of art, imitation, and exercise may stand as much as an observation about who was able to produce poetry during the Renaissance as how it should be produced. High literary culture was the preserve, naturally, of the literate but also of those educated within a classical tradition, acquainted with previous literary models. The appropriation of the past and its re-deployment through the creative process of imitation, presupposes an acquaintance with the literary canons of the past. Imitation in the Renaissance was practised as a dialogue with the past, where a text's individual distinctions was founded on its relation, both similarities and dissimilarities, with other earlier texts. To participate in such textual production in either a critical or creative fashion required an educative process open to relatively few. Exercise assumes writers with enough leisure to practise their art and with access to writing material. For the majority these facilities were

---

[1] See Margreta de Grazia, 'The Essential Shakespeare and the material book', *Textual Practice*, 2, 1, (1988), pp. 69–86; Terrence Hawkes, 'Telmah', in Patricia Parker and Geoffrey Hartman (eds) *Shakespeare and the Question of Theory* (New York, Methuen, 1985), pp. 310–32; 'Part II Reproductions, interventions' of *Political Shakespeare*, op. cit., esp. pp. 130–201 (see Preface, p. 3, note 1).

not readily available. Paper, for instance, was not cheap during the Renaissance. The Renaissance writer, therefore, is predominantly male, from a reasonably affluent background, and comparatively well educated. Most of the writing assumes a similar audience. In his letter to Sir Walter Ralegh explaining *The Faerie Queene*, Spenser argues the work is designed to 'fashion a gentleman or noble person' (p. 15). Spenser is thinking of a class of person within a distinctive social framework. His audience is not intended to be general.

Our literary canons have largely been constructed on such Renaissance suppositions. Renaissance poetry (in Sidney's sense of seriously crafted eloquent language which could include prose) is perceived to be the province of the truly serious writer, and this is equated with elitism. The period's drama which was not seriously considered as literature until the Jacobean period (and then only selectively) has been critically absorbed to now belong to elite literature. Shakespeare's drama is celebrated for its poetry, a compliment that on the surface suggests ideologically neutral approval of its language, but which also belies suppositions about the attitudes the plays' language articulates. Annabel Patterson's recent *Shakespeare and the Popular Voice*, for instance, demonstrates how critical writers in subsequent centuries enforced a view of Shakespeare's plays as voicing the concerns of the social elite, insisting Shakespeare be perceived as within the sphere of the 'gentleman', a position Patterson powerfully challenges.[1]

Our study of literary texts is commonly based on a view that the most self-consciously crafted literature has the greatest claim to our attention. Thus, a use of eloquent formal language, a confident employment of a literary heritage, and a preoccupation with either metaphysical themes or the large issues of state of especial interest to those in the governing classes are normally upheld as critical sign-posts directing us to the period's 'greatest' writing. In contrast a sub-genre such as domestic tragedy, of which the Renaissance period is filled with wonderfully rich examples, receives much less critical attention than

[1] Annabel Patterson, *Shakespeare and the Popular Voice* (Cambridge, Mass., Basil Blackwell, 1989).

those tragedies which deal with kings. That many domestic plays are often representations of actual events is seen to reduce their claims for attention because they do not deal with issues centred on a powerful elite employing language with rhetorical refinement. For every one current reader of *Arden of Faversham* there will be ten or more of *Tamburlaine* or *The Spanish Tragedy*. Yet, it is certainly possible to argue *Arden* is as dramatically interesting. *Arden*, certainly, is as culturally revealing.

Spenser could consider himself a gentleman only on the basis of having been to university and acquired a Master of Arts degree. His work is filled with a hatred of savagery, of ungovernable elements in both self and state. Ben Jonson, a 'scholarship boy' whose ability with language allowed him to gain social advancement, is keen to distance himself from popular writing whose techniques he so skilfully employs. Both Spenser's and Jonson's social aspirations, geared to their ability to use language, indicates a desire to see educated cultural expression indicating a class standing, a social elitism on the part of those who participate in cultural pursuits. It is noticeable the way current academia has developed its own critical strategies to suggest it, too, wishes to participate in a social elite. The educated are imagined as those who read and study something different, more *advanced*, than what the masses do. There often appears unconsciously held suppositions that superior literary writings will deal with issues divorced from ordinary concerns or at least adopt a perspective of the ordinary which is shared by the social elite.

Compare the following two expressions of humility in addressing the divine from George Herbert and from the mid-seventeenth-century poet An Collins:

> Who says that fictions only and false hair
> Become a verse? Is there in truth no beauty?
> Is all good structure in a winding stair?
> May no lines pass, except they do their duty
>   Not to a true, but painted chair?
>
> Is it no verse, except enchanted groves
> And sudden arbours, shadow coarse-spun lines?
> Must purling streams refresh a lovers loves?
> Must all be veiled, while he that reads, divines,
>   Catching the sense at two removes?

Shepherds are honest people; let them sing:
Riddle who list, for me, and pull for prime:
I envy no man's nightingale or spring;
Nor let them punish me with loss of rhyme,
   Who plainly say, *My God, My King*.

George Herbert, Jordan (1)[1]

Now touching that I hasten to expresse
Concerning these, the offspring of my mind,
Who though they here appeare in homly dresse
And as they are my works, I do not find
But ranked with others, they may go behind,
Yet for theyr matter, I suppose they bee
Not worthless quite, whilst they with Truth agree.

Indeed I grant that sounder judgements may
(Directed by a greater Light) declare
The ground of Truth more in a Gospel-way,
But who time past with present will compare
Shall find more mysteries unfolded are,
So that they may who have right informacion
More plainly shew the path-way to Salvacion.

(An Collins, from The Preface to
Divine Songs and Meditacions)[2]

Herbert's poem ostensibly contrasts the elaborations of secular verse with the straightforward quality of divine celebration. Yet his conclusion is hardly straightforward. He, of course, has not lost rhyme with his plain saying – his final line fits comfortably into his structure. But, further, his plain remark: 'My God, My King' is not the spontaneous exaltation he pretends. Herbert is using the language of Scripture. His statement is also that of Psalm 68 (verse 24) where the presence of my God and my King in the sanctuary is not plain but celebrated in a rich display of singers, musicians, and 'damsels playing with timbrels'. The skilfully deployed irony in Herbert's case is enhanced by the Psalm's announcement of God's punishment of those who are his people's enemies, rather than the reverse as Herbert's poem suggests. But what is most striking is that by adopting the voice of the Psalm, Herbert is also adopting the voice of a king (and a shepherd) as the

[1] Louis L. Martz (ed.) *George Herbert and Henry Vaughan*, The Oxford Authors (Oxford, Oxford University Press, 1986), pp. 48–9.
[2] In Greer, *Kissing the Rod*, op. cit., pp. 148–9.

Psalm was presented as being authored by a divinely inspired King David. Despite Herbert's claim to be using the plain saying of direct felt expression and humility towards addressing the divine, he is also demonstrating his poetic standing. Not only does his poem bring attention to its control of verse, Herbert signals a poetic origin for his expression which is regal and divinely sanctioned. Those who would punish him must deny Scripture, and Scripture indicates it is they who will be the ones punished.

An Collins's verse is far less cleverly constructed. Its expression of humility is made with distinct poetic self-effacement. Her claims to be heard are based on her spiritual topic matter and the historical accident that she writes at a time when she believes more has been revealed about the divine and therefore she possesses 'more information' than previously. She does not claim any immediate spiritual direction. Herbert's piece radiates confidence in its control of language and its message. It is a wonderful example of learned eloquence considering the problems associated with writing poetry and spiritual expression as befits a man who was a Cambridge University Praelector in Rhetoric and University Orator. Collins does not make poetic claims, nor does her use of language demonstrate the clever turns and plays of Herbert. Herbert would seem to be far more obviously the choice for literary study, and the institutional canon confirms this. Herbert is widely read, where Collins is seldom even heard of.

At the beginning of her Preface to *Divine Songs and Meditacions*, Collins claims she undertook to write: 'Being through weakness to the house confin'd/My mental powers seeming long to sleep'.[1] The remarks probably refer to illness, but they stand in a metaphoric sense for the condition that Renaissance women usually confronted. Collins's weakness is the patriarchal designated weakness of her sex which debars her from participation in public life outside the household. The benefits of education were rarely extended to women. As a sex, women joined other culturally disenfranchised groups who could not easily participate in high culture. The cultural practice of imitation which Herbert so confidently exploits (note how the

[1] Ibid., p. 148.

Jordan poem above skilfully employs Sidney's first sonnet in *Astrophil and Stella*) was rendered very difficult for a poet such as An Collins whose scope for enjoying the educated attainments open to a Renaissance gentleman was neglible.

Those writing from below, however, also eagerly sought to employ imitation, even if their range of prior texts was circumscribed. They, too, believed that a previous voice could be made their own. The Ranter Jacob Bauthumley begins his tract on *The Light and Dark side of God* acknowledging 'the most unto whose hand it [i.e. the tract] may come cannot read it'.[1] Yet, Bauthumley felt his own humble social position was one which gave his voice special importance:

> And however my person, and parts be meane in the Worlds Eye, and so may cast an odium upon the things that I hold forth; yet I shall runne the hazard in that kinde, and leave the Lord to gain his own Honour and Glory in it; as seeing by sweet experience, it is one of his greatest designes in the World, to confound the high and mighty things thereof, by the most meane and contemptible.

(p. 228)

The meanness of his voice makes it particularly appropriate to his audience, because Bauthumley holds up his own discourse as a model for the voices of those who are normally rendered silent:

> there are some . . . that travell with me in the same birth; yet are not able to bring forth their conceptions, for so much as many times, the Truth suffers by a weake delivery; and for their sakes have I held this Glasse before them, that so they may be the better able to describe themselves to others; and to help them to bring forth that out of their mouths, which perhaps may lye in the bottome of their hearts.

(p. 229)

Imitation did not only engage those involved in creating the fictional truths of sophisticated culture. At a popular level the emphasis of the individual's response to Scripture prompted by the Protestant Reformation allowed biblical

[1] In *A Collection of Ranter Writings*, op. cit., p. 228. All citations from Bauthumley are from this edition.

imitation to dominate the discourse of socially and culturally disenfranchised men and women. Bauthumley, who
believes God speaks directly through him, offers his own
writing as an imitative model to others 'that travell with me
in the same birth'. Similarly, the mid-seventeenth-century
prophetess, Anna Trapnel stresses that her discourse is
that of God, gathered from Scripture and not her own.
When being questioned by magistrates about her teaching
(they were suspicious of her on the grounds of her sex
and lack of social position) she is confident that a greater
Lord will answer for her. She places her trust in another's
voice:

> as for my going before the rulers, I was no whit afraid or
> thoughtful, for I had cast my care upon the Lord, which
> I was persuaded would speak for me. therefore I was not
> troubled nor afraid, for the Lord said to me, 'Fear not, be
> not dismayed, I am thy God, and will stand by thee'
> (Isaiah 41:10)[1]

Trapnel's example brings attention to a distinctive
problem about the nature of imitative voice which sepa-
rates the culturally disenfranchised from those culturally empowered through education in formal eloquence.
Writers within a high culture framework self-consciously
employ a literary past to create a distinctive contemporary
utterance of their own.[2] Imitation gives them individual
voice. In contrast, figures outside the high cultural sphere
often consciously try to abandon their sense of self. The
authority of their voice is gained by it being that of another,
almost always that of God, whose voice is more powerful
than those of the social institutions they see ranged against
them. Trapnel recounts how during her questioning by
local magistrates in Cornwall a large crowd gathered:

> the rude multitude said, 'Sure this woman is no witch,
> for she speaks many good words, which the witches
> could not'. And thus the Lord made the rude rabble to
> justify his appearance. For in all that was said by me, I
> was nothing, the Lord put all in my mouth, and told me

---

[1] From *Anna Trapnel's Report and Plea*, in Elspeth Graham, Hilary Hinds, Elaine Hobby, Helen
Wilcox (eds) *Her Own Life: Autobiographical Writings by Seventeenth-century Englishwomen*
(London, Routledge, 1989), p. 78. All citations from Trapnel are from this edition.
[2] Jean-Claude Carron, 'Imitation and intertextuality in the Renaissance', *New Literary
History*, 19 (1988), pp. 565–79.

what I should say, and that from the written word, he put it in my memory and mouth; so that I will have nothing ascribed to me.

(p. 84)

Here then, it is not only Trapnel's voice which is directed by God, but also the voices of the multitude. The commonalty find their justification in speaking by speaking as the mouthpiece of another.

Traditional literary criticism has celebrated the growth of the vernacular as a vehicle for expression during the Renaissance. Milton's *Paradise Lost* or Spenser's *Faerie Queene* are applauded for bringing a sophisticated use of classical epic conventions into English, creating national works which stand comparison with those of antiquity. Yet, traditional criticism has generally been uninterested in the widening of vernacular expression among groups previously unable to record their voices. Bauthumley's or Trapnel's texts record a different type of vernacular writing from high cultural expression; but the desire for voice, gained by imitation of approved previous writing, is a phenomenon which they too share in.

We are increasingly becoming aware of the interaction between high and popular culture, and how the Renaissance does not exclusively separate the two. In doing so the literary canon is forced to change. We can no longer smugly claim that literary criticism is concerned only with 'the best' expression of the period, because what is best is dependent on a host of preconceptions about what we wish to learn about Renaissance writing. An Collins's expression of self-effacing humility is *better* than Herbert's in the sense that Collins's humility is paramount where Herbert is maintaining a strong concept of self and, indeed, self-applause. We return to the need to make the questions we ask of Renaissance literature distinct. If we claim our interest is to focus on the writing produced only by a sophisticated elite, and that we determine the best literature is that which, in terms of generic structure, subject, and eloquent rhetoric, concerns itself with the preoccupations of males who have a high social and political standing, then the traditional canon will serve the majority of our needs. But if our interests are increasingly focused on different types of expression across a wide social framework, for instance if we are concerned to pursue the dissemination of vernacular innovation across the whole social spectrum, then our previous canons will prove inadequate. Bauthumley's or Trapnel's literary sophistication is limited, yet their writing as cultural documents are as important as Herbert's. The resistance to Bauthumley or Trapnel as figures worthy of study is part of an institutional assumption that literary study in higher education should force a separation between the elite and the popular, the sophisticated and the simplistic.

Spenser was able to use his MA to call himself a gentleman, his education was the key to his social mobility. The equation between study in higher education and social mobility still holds in curiously similar ways. By selecting a canon of texts which reflect the preoccupations of elite culture there is a presumption that the student is being initiated into some form of elite culture whose distinction from popular culture must be enforced. In Britain, this has usually meant that 'serious' books from the past have formed the core of degree work in English. Pre-twentieth-century poetic texts have commonly been at the core of syllabuses in the older universities, whereas the novel and more contemporary writing are commonly at the centre (or at least imagined by many in the academic establishment to be the centre) of course structures within the newer universities and polytechnics, institutions which are also usually viewed as less socially elite. Given the structure of the traditional canon, this has regrettably meant that Renaissance writing was employed to mark out a high cultural orientation. In a battle between ancients and moderns which is frequently waged in English departments, Renaissance writing is too often perceived at the centre of the argument for the preservation of a restrictive high cultural ethos in literary study. As I hope I have demonstrated, though, this should not automatically be the case. To evaluate Renaissance writing as only the expression of a cultural elite means being highly selective when choosing what material should be studied. There are other texts which answer different needs, both our own and those living at the time the texts were produced. This is not to imply that expressions of sophisticated learned eloquence should be abandoned in favour of popular writing. I have tried to show that our experience of the Renaissance is enriched by comparing texts produced in a variety of cultural environments. Ranter writing should not displace *Paradise Lost*; *Arden of Faversham* and domestic tragedy should not merely replace *The Spanish Tragedy* and court-centred drama. What we require are canonical structures which allow our study of the Renaissance to include texts which speak, to use Bauthumley's words, for those things 'meane and contemptible' as well as for those 'high and mighty'.

4

The New Historicism

I

Some of the changes to our critical practice which results
from incorporating new models for thinking about the relation between Renaissance literary texts and their historical
context can be illustrated by considering a sonnet by Sir
Thomas Wyatt:

> Each man me telleth I change most my device,
> And on my faith me think it good reason
> To change propose like after the season,
> For in every case to keep still one guise
> Is meet for them that would be taken wise:
> And I am not of such manner condition,
> But treated after a diverse fashion,
> And thereupon my diverseness doth rise.
> But you that blame this diverseness most,
> Change you no more, but still after one rate
> Treat ye me well, and keep ye in the same state:
> And while with me doth dwell this wearied ghost,
> My word nor I shall not be variable,
> But always one, your own both firm and stable.[1]

This can be viewed as a familiar meditation on the theme
of constancy and inconstancy between lovers, the reader
being granted a glimpse into a private world whose terms
of precise reference remain unknown. But the sonnet also
provides a glimpse into the dilemmas of identity the
Renaissance articulated. The sonnet stands not only as
an account of some private instance but as a representative
account of the pressures and inevitable containment of
individuals by powerful forces outside their control. Wyatt
answers the charge that he alters his device (his project and
designs but also his heraldic sign – the symbolic means
by which he announces his public identity) by using the
analogy of changing seasons to suggest mutability is an

[1] Joost Daalder (ed.), *Sir Thomas Wyatt: Collected Poems* (London, Oxford University
Press, 1975), p. 14. I am grateful to Jonathan Sawday for bringing this poem to my
attention.

inevitable and indeed appropriate condition. His defence
of his 'diverness' is that this is the way he experiences the
world, others treat him differently all the time (especially
the figure addressed in the sonnet) and he responds in
kind. He would be immutable in his relation with the
addressee if she/he did not change. Wyatt's defence of his
accommodation with the world reflects, though, the harsh
conditions which enforce such accommodation if existence
is to continue. 'Change you no more' has the provocation of
a challenge not expected to be accepted. Existence depends
on mutability because the conditions of the world make
the maintenance of 'one guise' impossible. Those who are
'wise' may keep to one purpose, but the implication is that
such wisdom is not allowed to exist for very long. The poet's
claim that he will readily participate in any form of stability
his lover settles on is accompanied by the qualification that
he will do so only as long as 'this wearied ghost' dwells in
him. Refusal to change your outward 'device' is likely to
lead to a permanent rest.

Wyatt's articulation of the necessity to stage his identity,
even within the ostensible private world of a sonnet, so that
he can continue to function within the social world is reiter-
ated by writers whose focus is more distinctly on the pubic
sphere. In his life of *Richard III* Thomas More noted how
The Duke of Buckingham in offering the crown to Richard
in 1484 at Baynard's Castle assumed a role in a staged
presentation in which Richard feigned reluctance in accepting the offer of kingship. The spectators knew that the
whole event was a staged act and yet complied: 'because all
must be done in good order'.[1] Order and obedience to the
crown were commonplace principles which popular moral
writing constantly rehearsed throughout the Middle Ages
and Renaissance. Even in rebellion, as Mervyn James has
noted of the Lincolnshire rebellions of 1536 against Henry
VIII, the rebels maintained they were loyal to the king.[2]
The appearance of obedience, even when the participants
engaged in actions which were expressly otherwise, was
a compelling necessity. The reasons behind playing this

[1] Sir Thomas More, *The History of King Richard III*, R. S. Sylvester (ed.) *The Complete
Works of St Thomas More*, vol. 3 (New Haven, Yale University Press, 1963), p. 80.
[2] Mervyn James, 'Obedience and dissent in Henrician England: the Lincolnshire rebellion,
1536', in *Society, Politics and Culture: Studies in Early Modern England* (Cambridge,
Cambridge University Press, 1986), pp. 188–269.

game were not based only on an abstract conception of duty, but also on the notions expressed in More's conclusion to the stage managing which offered Richard III the crown:

> these matters be king's games, as it were stage plays, and for the more part played upon scaffolds. In which poor men be but the lookers-on. And they that wise be will meddle no farther. For they that sometime step up and play with them, when they cannot play their parts, they disorder the play and do themselves no good.[1]

The appearance of obedience was difficult to maintain in Tudor times when the terms on which it was founded were not clear. Reviewing recent historiography of the Reformation, Christopher Haigh has pointed out the constantly shifting conflicts between factions which existed in the English court between 1527 and 1553.[2] In such conflicts, Haigh notes, religious policy, on which obedience could be crucially tested, became both a weapon and a prize. At any number of points events could have developed in dramatically different ways if the balance of power had shifted only slightly.

Thomas More played his part upon a scaffold. He was one of those whose wisdom (to recall the terms of Wyatt's sonnet) insisted on his maintaining an unchanged obedience to an authority he ultimately felt to be higher than the King's. Wyatt's worldly recognition that his 'device' needed to be changed if he was to continue through the seasons is likely also to have been learned through his parts in kings' games. He was twice imprisoned when his loyalties were suspected. But it was not only writers with established political identities who were wary about how writing might be perceived. In general, most Renaissance texts were open to being co-opted into a part in these royal games (the term usefully suggests the way private activities such as sexual intrigues were more expressly combined with public political questions during the Renaissance). Even those texts which appeared concerned with uncontroversial matters were open to be

[1] More, *History of King Richard III*, op. cit. pp. 80–81.
[2] Christopher Haigh, 'The recent historiography of the English Reformation', in Christopher Haigh (ed.) *The English Reformation Revised* (Cambridge, Cambridge University Press, 1987), pp. 19–33.

seen as engaging in political and social questions in which the state could suddenly intervene and cause uneasy writers to account for their work. At the end of the sixth book of *The Faerie Queene*, Spenser alludes to the troubles some of his earlier work has caused through slanders which provoked 'a mighty Peres displeasure'. Spenser fears the same fate may await *The Faerie Queene* – 'this homely verse, of many meanest' – and commands his 'rimes' to keep measure and 'seeke to please, that now is counted wisemens threasure' (VI, XII, 41). In these circumstances, the familiar Renaissance claim that poetry teaches and delights takes on new implications, pleasure among readers is not only how their attention and co-option to the didactic intention is achieved. Pleasure also becomes the element which protects the poet from the action of the powerful against a message they may not be fully in agreement with. As Wyatt's sonnet indicates, even in the ostensibly private address of the sonnet, writing registered its uneasiness about the nature of its voice. One of Wyatt's 'devices' are the writings by which he is known, and they too must be open to seasonal change as is fitting the conditions of survival.

Considering literary texts not as autonomous utterances out of history, but as illustrations of a Renaissance culture whose forms of representation are conditioned by the social, political world they participate in has prompted readings of texts which seek to restore their former agencies and original discursive energies. But how do we gain access to Renaissance culture, especially when our readings of the texts that document that culture indicate that a process of necessary counterfeit may have played a part in determining how these texts inscribed their culture? The processes through which we can see texts functioning within a social and cultural context are problematic. Even more difficult is determining the methods through which wider cultural analysis can be employed. This chapter seeks to examine some of the means employed by New Historicism in trying to address these problems.

The term New Historicism has come in for considerable hostile criticism both from those who claim that there is nothing particularly new about it and among those who admire new historial methods but feel the term incorrectly suggests a unified theoretical field and subsequent critical practice within a body of critical writing in which much contending diversity exists. While both these objections have truth to them, it is also clear that a range of critical writings which share more preoccupations than differences has emerged and that it can be contrasted to other forms of writing about texts and history. I want to examine aspects of those preoccupations and ignore differences which are of varying orders rather than of kind. In particular, I will elide some of the different orientations between British Cultural Materialism and New Historicism in its more distinctly American guise.[1] My reasons for doing so are twofold. First, sub-divisions would only serve to create the appearance of a more precisely demarcated critical field than is in fact the case. Jonathan Dollimore's and Alan Sinfield's collection *Political Shakespeare: New Essays in Cultural Materialism*, for example, contains work by writers whose same essays in other contexts are labelled New Historicist. Second, the scope of what New Historicism involves is continuously changing, and the conflicts between contending views are often localised over a few issues. I do not want to ignore the wood for the sake of labelling all the trees. But, in the following discussions, I do take two leading new historicist writers, Louis Montrose and Stephen Greenblatt, as representing the current field, so it is probably inevitable that they will appear as paradigms for New Historicism as a whole. Many other writers working with similar concerns about the analysis of culture would wish to distance themselves from aspects of Montrose's and Greenblatt's orientation, though all would likely wish to acknowledge the influence of their work.

II

I intended to explore the ways in which major English writers of the sixteenth century created their own performances, to analyze the choices they made in representing

---

[1] For recent surveys of the two critical directions see H. Aram Veeser, 'Introduction', in *The New Historicism* op. cit., pp. ix–xvi (see Preface, note 3); Don E. Wayne, 'Power, politics, and the Shakespearean text: recent criticism in England and the United States', in Jean E. Howard and Marion F. O'Connor (eds) *Shakespeare Reproduced: the Text in History and Ideology* (New York, Methuen, 1987), pp. 47–67; Jonathan Dollimore, 'Shakespeare, cultural materialism, feminism and Marxist humanism', *New Literary History*, 21, 3 (1990), pp. 471–93.

themselves and in fashioning characters . . . but as my
work progressed, I perceived that fashioning oneself and
being fashioned by cultural institutions – family, religion,
state – were inseparably intertwined. In all my texts and
documents, there were, so far as I could tell, no moments
of pure, unfettered subjectivity; indeed, the human subject
itself began to seem remarkably unfree, the ideological
product of the relations of power in a particular socieity.[1]

Stephen Greenblatt's self-confessional epilogue to his
Renaissance Self-Fashioning which appeared in 1980 articulated a change of emphasis which marked out the
most pronounced critical practice of Renaissance literary
criticism in the past decade – the New Historicism. Where
Greenblatt, and most literary criticism of Renaissance
writing during the preceding decades, had formerly seen
one of the features of the period as the growing ability
for some individuals to shape their lives, there emerged
a recognition that Renaissance texts were not celebrating
human autonomy and unfettered subjectivity. Instead, a
new grouping of critics, working under the influence of
theorists such as Louis Althusser and Michel Foucault,
came to realise that literary texts did not mark out
expression which could somehow break free of the culture
which produced them. Texts were inevitably part of their
culture, as were the individuals who wrote them under
the shaping constraints of state, family, religion. Further,
these critics no longer imagined a culture which could be
ascertained only by examining selected artistic artefacts of
the period. What Renaissance culture was and how we
gain access to it increasingly became seen as problematic.
The idea that the Renaissance could be named, classified,
described, and interpreted so that it was rendered readily
comprehensible within some generalised scheme of the
humanities was no longer a clearly defined process.

Much of New Historical thought developed from the
impact of contemporary anthropological writing. Literary
critics began to see themselves in part as cultural historians responding to new processes advanced for the
understanding of culture by anthropologists, themselves

---

[1] Stephen Greenblatt, *Renaissance Self-Fashioning: From More to Shakespeare* (Chicago, The University of Chicago Press, 1980), p. 256.

using interdisciplinary methods to describe cultural phenomena. Indeed Stephen Greenblatt's preferred term for new historical activities, cultural poetics, more clearly indicates how anthropology rather than history has been the discipline which has more profoundly affected new historicist methods.[1] The argument advanced by the anthropologist Clifford Geertz that human societies needed to be interpreted as texts has been especially influential on New Historicist thought.[2] Anthropological inquiry into the meaning of cultures came to question the established categories which had provided the models and criteria to assess different cultures. Examining the cultural foundations through which societies characterised themselves (e.g. myths, rituals, games), anthropologists increasingly perceived that history is culturally ordered and produced according to the structures by which historical happenings are understood. Further, responding to the work of the French thinker Michel Foucault, scholars began to realise that projecting cultural order implies both rule *and* *transgression*.[3] The unfamiliar and the different is important for a generation of cultural meaning. Cultural artefacts and occurrences often previously perceived on the margins of what constituted the culture – for example how a culture defined and treated insanity – were recognised as an aid in revealing a great deal about the cultural orders celebrated at a society's centre (e.g. the way court ceremony was enacted).

Through theoretical inquiries into how cultural constructions are made, it became increasingly obvious to those working across a number of disciplines that historical events were no longer simply things that happened. An historical event was seen to be constructed from a number of different 'happenings' perceived as having specific meanings. The historical event, therefore, becomes a relation between a given symbolic system projected by

---

[1] *Shakespearean Negotiations*, op. cit., pp. 5–6 (see Chapter 3, note 1); Stephen Greenblatt, 'Towards a Poetics of Culture', in *The New Historicism*, op. cit., pp. 1–14 (see Preface, note 3).

[2] See particularly, Clifford Geertz, *The Interpretation of Cultures* (New York, Basic Books, 1973).

[3] See for example the anthropologist James Clifford, *The Predicament of Culture* (Cambridge, Mass., Harvard University Press, 1988) especially 'On Ethnographic Surrealism', pp. 117–53; for literary application see Peter Stallybrass and Allon White, *The Politics and Poetics of Transgression* (London, Methuen, 1986).

a cultural scheme and a certain happening.[1] This is not to suggest that history only happens because some later critic constructs it. Things do, of course, happen. There are real sets of occurrences possessed of objective properties. But to describe the effects of history, to give happenings meanings so they become seen as events – as happenings within a decided structure – requires that these happenings are projected from a specific cultural scheme which gives them their significance. As we saw in chapter 2, new concerns with linguistic structures revealed that much of our understanding of 'things' in language rested on accepting given structures which language in itself did not necessarily support. Similarly, anthropologists and cultural historians came to realise that our understanding of culture had rested on *a priori* concepts and categories. We assessed a culture by describing its perceived contexts through our received categories.

Anthropologists such as Clifford Geertz or Marshall Sahlins exploring the cultural manifestations of the Balinese or of South Sea islanders projected interpretations of these cultures which could be read as stories the people of these societies tell about themselves.[2] Cultural acts and rituals could be interpreted as texts which reveal the sense of a society's ordering and structuring of experience. Sahlins, for instance, discussed the way the Hawaiian Islanders experienced the visit of Captain Cook, placing it within their own received cultural categories to give the empirical happening of Cook's arrival a meaning.[3] The reality of Cook's visit came to be understood through a relation of the practical reference (the ships arriving) and the cultural sense (what the ships' arrival meant according to existing categories for interpreting experience). Sahlins then paralleled the British understanding of the same events, again constructed out of their cultural categories reacting to the perceived contexts. Importantly, Sahlins does not privilege one perspective over the other: the British perspective is not treated as better or more informed because to

[1] The ideas are expanded at length by Marshall Sahlins, *Islands of History* (London, Tavistock Publications, 1987), esp. pp. 144–54.
[2] For a consideration of both Geertz and Sahlins see Aletta Biersack, 'Local knowledge, local history: Geertz and beyond', in Lynn Hunt (ed.) *The New Cultural History* (Berkeley, University of California Press, 1989), pp. 72–96.
[3] Sahlins, *Islands of History*, op. cit.

treat it as such would be to accept unquestioningly the categories out of which this perspective constructed its realities. Sahlins' point is to show how to both sides differing types of sense were formed of what Cook's arrival 'meant'. This type of analysis forces a recognition of a greater diversity of structures by which history may be written and understood. For Sahlins demonstrates how the obscure histories of remote islanders take a place alongside our self-contemplations of a European past – a supposed history of civilisation – for their own contributions to a historical understanding.[1] It is no longer possible to make claims to understand a culture simply by classifying it in terms of its relations to a present western culture. Geertz's study of Balinese culture led him to conclude:

> The culture of a people is an ensemble of texts, themselves ensembles which the anthropologist strains to read over the shoulders of those to whom they properly belong. There are enormous difficulties in such an enterprise, methodological pitfalls . . . and some moral perplexities as well . . . But to regard such [cultural] forms as 'saying something of something', and saying it to somebody, is at least to open up the possibility of an analysis which attends to their substance rather than to reductive formulas professing to account for them.[2]

The anthropologist's task, therefore, is to gain access to societies through means which contain these societies' own interpretations about themselves. As Geertz recognises this is a potentially difficult task as the reader of a society is to some extent an intruder and capable of serious misreadings. Cultural readers, of course, inevitably respond in terms of their own cultural preoccupations.

New Historicism in Renaissance studies responded to this awareness that an understanding of a culture was created by an examination of perceived contexts and received categories by questioning previous boundaries and classifications in which literary texts were examined. Many of New Historicism's endeavours are shared by the wider questioning of practice that is taking place in a variety of disciplines and theoretical approaches. New Historicism

---

[1] Ibid., p. 72.
[2] Clifford Geertz, 'Deep play: notes on the Balinese cock fight', in Clifford Geertz (ed.) *Myth, Symbol, and Culture* (New York, W. W. Norton, 1974), p. 29.

recognises that literary and non-literary texts circulate inseparably in a society. It perceives that an expressive act is embedded in a network of material practices within a given culture. A limited example of this is the recognition that whether a text is published in quarto or folio or whether it circulates as a manuscript will help to create the conditions in which the text's meaning is understood within a given culture at a particular historical instant. Not surprisingly then, New Historicism accepts that no discourse gives access to unchanging truths. In fact, New Historicism resists claims that large-scale generalisations about a whole culture can be confidently made. It claims to be a critical practice not an organised theoretical doctrine. It is often sceptical of an insistence on any one theoretical model – believing, for instance, that both Marxists and post-structuralists use history as a convenient ornament to hang upon their respective theoretical structures. In their own self-analysis, New Historians have emphasised as strengths their recognition that social and cultural events in a society commingle messily and to offer a coherent account of their relations is difficult.[1] Further, New Historicism is aware that every critique which purports to demystify previous critical models relies to some extent on existing structures and, therefore, risks creating new ones which fall prey to the very practices supposedly being exposed. Most New Historical writing on the Renaissance has openly acknowledged the difficulties inherent in reading texts as cultural documents. Louis Montrose, who has become New Historicism's most eloquent theoretical exponent, has described the self-critical awareness which prompts a new relation between texts and history as based on:

> a reciprocal concern with the historicity of texts and the textuality of history. By *the historicity of texts*, I mean to suggest the cultural specificity, the social embedment, of all modes of writing. . . . By the *textuality of history*, I mean to suggest, firstly, that we can have no access to a full and authentic past, a lived material existence, unmediated by the surviving textual traces of the society in question – traces whose survival we cannot assume to be merely contingent but must rather presume to be at least partially

---

[1] H. Aram Veeser, 'Introduction', *The New Historicism*, op. cit., p. xiii.

consequent upon complex and subtle social processes of preservation and effacement; and secondly, that those textual traces are themselves subject to subsequent textual mediations when they are construed as the 'documents' upon which historians ground their own texts, called histories.[1]

New Historicism is, therefore, fundamentally concerned to be aware of its critical project and considers that any inquiry into the past must be based upon a current critical partiality which marks out the inquisitor's history. It has, not surprisingly, been at the forefront of critical enterprises which have considered literature's different relations with history that we explored in the first chapter.

Montrose's chiastic formulation of the historicity of texts and the textuality of history (chiasmus is a rhetorical balancing created by the reversal of one concept by that succeeding it) is indicative of some of the problems New Historicism's methods share with the anthropological methods for reading cultures which New Historicism adopted. Montrose's formulation is rhetorically neat but its application could be expected to produce results which are conflicting and disruptive. The historicity of texts might reasonably be thought to produce readings which are difficult to incorporate with the textuality of history. As we understand more about a text's specific historicity, how it emerged from a distinctive social embedment, we might expect it to be unavailable sometimes for current employment. The process by which a text participates in the textuality of history is, as Montrose acknowledges, a process of effacement as well as preservation. If we recover more of a text's historicity, recapture the lost agencies which originally motivated its emergence and come to understand more about the conditions of its emergence, we may find a cultural presence strange and apparently remote from our own. The processes through which the text has become part of the textuality of history will probably have meant the re-deployment of those original agencies so that they have reappeared in some disguised fashion within currently familiar structural organisation for understanding culture. The New Historicists' 'reciprocal

[1] Louis A. Montrose, 'Professing the Renaissance: the poetics and politics of culture', ibid., p. 20.

concern with the historicity of texts and the textuality of history' would set up an exchange which might be assumed to be awkward. Since historicity and textuality are no longer imagined as smooth pegs sliding into smooth holes, but are seen as irregular and variable-sided, fitting them together will presumably involve some difficulty. In New Historicism this awkwardness should not be deplored but seen as proof of the integrity of its methods.

In practice, though, Montrose's neat formulation of the historicity of texts and the textuality of history reveals the characteristic roundness and balance through which New Historicist readings are conducted. It may seem paradoxical, but New Historicism's acknowledgement of a great complexity and subtlety between text and history and its hesitancy to make generalised claims for a culture has so far produced critical analysis of texts which tend to be recognisably similar to one another.[1] Discovery of a text's more specific historical embedment usually finds it confronting issues which are comfortably familiar, if usually unwelcome, to a late twentieth century social and political perspective. Further, the range of issues highlighted in the texts and their cultural specificity which have so far been those approached by New Historicism are relatively small, giving the appearance of relatively unified Renaissance cultural preoccupations.

New Historicism, thus, seems to ignore many of the premises it claims to operate on. While on the one hand claiming to recognise the theoretical problems inherent in classifying cultural features and the possibility of interpreting otherwise, New Historicist writing tends to produce very organised, well-constructed and argued cases for a small number of Renaissance cultural features. Inevitably, New Historicist case studies of specific texts and specific contexts start to feel like metaphors for the whole culture. Although, claiming that they bring attention to their own historicity, New Historicists are reluctant to map out what that historicity is. In other words, the type of critical and political self-analysis which New Historicists claim to be aware of is insufficiently foregrounded when reading a Renaissance text. Claims for a personalised

[1] For a good critique of this see James Holstun, 'Ranting at the New Historicism', *English Literary Renaissance*, 19, 2 (1989), pp. 189–225.

critical engagement are made, such as Stephen Greenblatt's opening to *Shakespearean Negotiations*:

> I began with the desire to speak with the dead. This desire is a familiar, if unvoiced motive in literary study, a motive organised, professionalised, buried beneath thick layers of bureaucratic decorum: literature professors are salaried middle-class shamans. If I never believed the dead could hear me, and if I knew that the dead could not speak, I was nonetheless certain that I could re-create a conversation with them.[1]

But if Greenblatt recognises that he believes 'literature professors are salaried, middle-class shamans', he is reluctant to confront his position as shaman.

One of the disconcerting features of New Historicist accounts is that a recognition of critical partially and a mapping out of the historicity of texts through the textuality of history does not produce a critical manner which is careful and self-scrutinising. Rather the critic frequently seems to adopt an inflated posture, where his or her negotiation of a text becomes a journey of discovery marked out with a rhetoric of almost heroic endeavour. It can make excellent reading but its ordered narrative can create the impression of a unified cultural field which it is sometimes difficult to see beyond. If Montrose chiastic formulation (historicity of texts/textuality of history) suggests an expected critical process which is not balanced but open to intrusions, constant qualification and, in effect, cultural deconstruction, what is more frequently produced is a critical narrative which creates an impression of cultural chiasmus, a balance in which the reciprocal concerns between original cultural embedment and subsequent textual mediations are equally suspended. The result is a circulation between past and present which flows easily. But should it?

One of the methodologies used by anthropology is 'thick description', the telling at great length of some cultural occurrence, one in which the anthropologist is frequently involved, followed by its analysis. The 'thick description' takes on a type of metaphoric quality: it stands as a symbolic indication of some wider social meaning within the culture which is elicited through critical interpretation. Clifford

---

[1] *Shakespearean Negotiations*, op. cit., p. 1.

Geertz's widely known article on 'Deep Play: Notes on the Balinese Cockfight' which is both an account of the way cockfighting may be seen as a symbolically charged text acting as a 'carefully prepared' expression of Balinese life and an account of the processes by which Geertz becomes a knowing reader of this text, is a prime example of the way thick description works.[1] The article betrays a great deal, not only in the way it constructs its narrative, but in what it omits and suppresses. What it does do very obviously is to construct a narrative, and a very readable one. Although it stands as an important account of new anthropological theory and purports to throw a revealing light on the social organisation of Balinese society, its carefully organised narrative is also a good story arranged so the shifts between Geertz's account of his gradual development as an *aficionado* of cockfighting and the development of his theory of the social significance of this sport merge. His narrative reveals Geertz (almost) capable of being a player himself, helping to establish his credibility as a knowing 'reader' of cockfighting and supporting his claims for the activity's wider anthropological significance. The authority of Geertz's claims is supported by the article's narrative structure which combine the rigours and difficulties attendant upon Geertz's introduction into a Balinese village– 'my wife and I arrived, malarial and diffident' – with the rigours of his intellectual inquiries – 'methodological pitfalls to make a Freudian quake'.[2] By surmounting, so he tells us, one set of obstacles in being accepted by the Balinese, he also creates the rhetorical conditions where we are likely to favour a belief that he has surmounted the theoretical obstacles attended on his methodological discovery as well. The stylistic aplomb of the article may have us accepting the analogous links made between cockfighting and the totality of Balinese society without realising that these links are too fragmentary and partial to stand properly for the whole.

The wholeness of Geertz's cultural reading of the Balinese is achieved only by omission and suppression. For example, Geertz's wife is introduced in the article's opening section as a companion in his rigorous journey, but

[1] Geertz, 'Deep play', op. cit., pp. 1–37.
[2] Ibid., p. 1.

she rapidly disappears from the narrative.[1] It is noticeable that cockfighting is an exclusively male preoccupation, though this is not really analysed. Geertz's assertions about Balinese society emerge from the wholly male-dominated world of cockfighting. But just as Geertz's textually absent wife must have been present in reality, contributing to Geertz encounter with the Balinese, so women are also present in Balinese society though they may be absent from cockfighting. If Geertz is right that cockfighting is, perceived from a particular angle, an instance of how Balinese men imagined themselves to be, it is an imaginary projection Geertz too uncannily shares. Just as cockfighting allows a world where women are rendered invisible, so Geertz's writing creates a text where his actually present wife is ignored as a non-person. The point is that a careful reading of this fluent and apparently self-conscious critical analysis of a culture raises serious suspicions about the nature of its claims. What appears to work within the carefully structured world of the article seems to have a dubiously partial relation to what it represents about Balinese life as a whole.

Similarly, Marshall Sahlins's work on the Hawaiian islanders in his *Islands of History*, though far more acutely aware of contending multiple narratives trying to ascribe different significances to the same happenings, is also organised so that it allows Sahlins to present a narrative wherein conflicting stories/histories are mapped out in a framework which explores these histories' interpenetrations, their assimilations of each other rather than their refusals of each other. If some anthropologists, such as Geertz, are interested in the webs of significance humans spin for themselves, while others, such as Sahlins, are more focused on the processes of how those webs are spun, both groups reveal the central role of the interpreter in shaping the material to be represented and in organising the structures in which the representations occur.

Within New Historical writing the anecdote which symbolically reveals some important facet of Renaissance culture is a familiar critical practice. The best written New Historicism, and Stephen Greenblatt's work is particularly

[1] I am grateful to Sabina Sharkey for this insight.

exemplary, shows great skill in constructing a narrative. New Historicism is very adept at employing 'thick description', a detailed skilful exposition of, usually, some text or document which has been largely critically bypassed previously, but which is shown to have a charged metaphoric function in revealing some facet of Renaissance culture. The compelling analysis of this anecdote is then shown to have important implications for the reading of some familiar literary text, revealing that it too shares in the cultural presumptions critically uncovered in the anecdote. What emerges is the implication that the perceived cultural exchange between these selected texts reveal preoccupations found throughout the whole culture.

Greenblatt's *Shakespearean Negotiations*, for instance, is interested in the way the Elizabethan theatre produced texts which were in no respect outside other institutions of the time. Rather dramatic texts were 'literary creations designed in intimate and living relation to an emergent commercial practice'.[1] Greenblatt explores the ways a self-conscious theatricality permeated Elizabethan society at all levels: in its staging of royal pageants and progressions, in the celebrations of religious ritual, even in the performance of public executions. Greenblatt's project is to understand how works of art obtain and amplify powerful social energies. He proposes that we employ a notion of *energia*, that which stirs the mind, as the means through which texts are aesthetically empowered with 'life'. This energy's origins are in rhetoric, but its significance is both social and historical. A study of it leads us to witness a text's position within the social and cultural climate from which it emerged, and with which it negotiates. Recalling the Renaissance's preoccupation with mirrors and optics, in which an exchange – something moving back and forth between viewer and image – was postulated, Greenblatt proposes a similar procedure taking place with Shakespeare's texts. These negotiate with their age (and with subsequent ages) through a process of these mirror-like exchanges, ones which cover a whole spectrum of representations. We should not look for a simple reflection: 'a single, fixed mode of exchange; in reality there are many

---

[1] *Shakespearean Negotiations*, op. cit., p. 13.

modes, their character is determined historically, and they are continually renegotiated'.[1]

Greenblatt's explorations proceeds by a process of 'thick description', paralleling some of Shakespeare's plays with texts neither dramatic nor formally literary but which stand in symbolic relation to one another. Thus he considers *King Lear* and Samuel Harsnett's *A Declaration of Egregious Popish Impostures*, a text directly concerned with the theatrical manipulations found in contemporary exorcisms.[2] Harsnett's text has long been seen as one of the established sources for *Lear*, but in Greenblatt's analysis a more challenging question is posed: which way was the borrowing? Did Harsnett initially borrow from 'Shakespeare' (or his theatre) and *Lear* is, therefore, a borrowing back? Further, do the series of cultural negotiations which emerge from the two texts produce a larger 'cultural text' as a result of this exchange?

Harsnett's *Declaration* only formally supplies *Lear* with the model for Edgar's histrionic disguise as Poor Tom. In reading Greenblatt it can too often seem that discussions of such selective parts of a play may appear to stand for the whole. In this instance, Greenblatt does successfully illuminate a selective consideration in a manner which profitably and suggestively links it with larger issues the play addresses. As he illustrates, in Harsnett's case the theatre was a: 'symbolically charged zone of pollution, disease, and licentious entertainment'.[3] But it was one believed by Harsnett to be controlled by the state and at the periphery of society. By 'placing' exorcism in such a zone, state institutions (which Greenblatt equates with Harsnett's text) can attempt to contain what is potentially disruptive to the state; eliminating, in this case, charismatic religious groups as a potential threat to the established Church. Shakespeare negotiates with Harsnett's *Declaration*. He adopts Harsnett's premise that possession is a theatrical performance – Edgar continually brings attention to his madness being a pretence. But Shakespeare's manipulation ultimately disrupts Harsnett's design: 'In Shakespeare, the realization that demonic possession is

[1] Ibid., p. 8.
[2] Ibid., pp. 94–128.
[3] Ibid., p. 114.

a theatrical imposture leads not to a clarification – the clear-eyed satisfaction of a man who refuses to be gulled – but to a deeper uncertainty, a loss of moorings, in the face of evil.'[1]

For Greenblatt, *King Lear* is a play haunted by a sense of rituals and beliefs that have been emptied out. The play exposes the horror of a world which, drained of its rituals, is left exposed to a released and enacted wickedness neither its individuals nor its institutions can contain. The result is to cause us to love the theatre: 'the play recuperates and intensifies our need for these ceremonies, even though we do not believe in them, and performs them, carefully marked out for us as frauds, for our continued consumption'.[2] It is a conclusion about an almost psychiatric effect (and comfort) offered by serious drama which Aristotle would have had much sympathy with.

As a reading of *King Lear*, Greenblatt's is unquestionably very rewarding. But should we raise objections about a too selective use of examples, both within Shakespeare's plays – where they are often exclusively considered – and in the choice of texts which help detail the period's 'social energy'? Within the narrative of Greenblatt's discussion, the Harsnett text appears to assume a type of objective status as a uncontested point of historical reference, operating as a representative example for Elizabethan attitudes toward theatricality. Greenblatt does not explain why one 'historical' text is chosen rather than another, and whether they may, or may not be, considered representative of those commonly found in cultural circulation. This has been the frequent and characteristic complaint of those (in my experience few) historians who have explored the New Historicism: the representation of history is idiosyncratic and selected to reflect the preoccupation of the literary critic, not an attempt to account accurately for the period. New Historicism's usual response to this is to expand on Montrose's point about the inevitability of critical partiality existing. As we saw in chapter 1 'history' is largely an ideological construct. Critics and historians represent the past in terms of their own current concerns.

[1] Ibid., p. 122.
[2] Ibid., p. 128.

The problem is that New Historicism refuses or only very reluctantly foregrounds its own historicity and position within an ideology. For example in *Shakespearean Negotiations* Greenblatt discovers through a reading of Thomas Harriot's *Brief and True Report of the New Found Land of Virginia* and Shakespeare's *Henry V* the way actions which the state employs, and which should have a radically undermining effect, turn out to be props of authority. *King Lear* signals the implications and terrors of a demystified world. The work of a French doctor, Jacques Duval's *Des Hermaphordits, Twelfth Night* and *As You Like It* are the focus for an exploration of the ways a culture's sexual discourse plays a critical role in the shaping of identity. Discussion of work by Hugh Latimer and *The Tempest* considers the managing of anxiety by the state as a means of shaping and fashioning behaviour. These are all concerns central to our own current culture, and the essays help detail some of Shakespeare's negotiations with us as well as the possible 'social energy' of his own era. And nothing wrong in this. Each of these essays has important observations about these negotiations which enrich our experience of the plays. But if we seek through these texts to understand more about the social and cultural circulations of Renaissance England it becomes problematic. Questions about why *these* examples and not others constantly loom, because we can seriously doubt how representative the selected texts are.

Central to Greenblatt's readings is the argument of subversion and containment. It asks us to perceive Renaissance literature in a relation to the power exercised by the state's dominant political institutions. Literature is seen as often (perhaps unconsciously) acting in a subversive relation with such power, contending with it, questioning its norms. The real force of literature's subversive power, though, is ultimately contained because its texts are sanctioned by the state to play a subversive role, a role which state institutions can control. The argument is clearest in its application to the theatre: recall Harsnett's view that the theatre was a zone of pollution and licence, one capable of being managed by locating it in a designated place on the social periphery. The literary text may negotiate with its containment (as Shakespeare's do), but its contemporary subversive force has been compromised by the political dominance of state power which excludes it from the centre and places it on the margins of socially sanctioned institutions.

Greenblatt's inquiry into the 'half-hidden cultural trans-actions through which great works of art are empowered' uncovers a process by which Renaissance texts subvert but are then contained by state institutions.[1] But this reveals a cultural context of great importance only when we can be satisfied that his texts' historicity – their social embedment – is not determined by Greenblatt's own desire to keep these texts empowered. Could it be that New Histori-cists are only providing texts with a new textuality of history? New Historicists acting to ensure selected texts survive and are allowed to maintain their power? Con-sidering the use of the anecdote as a focus for analysis, Joel Fineman discusses the way anecdotes were used by Thucydides as *ta deonata*, the things necessary.[2] Anecdotes, Fineman argues, enabled the sentiments befitting the occa-sion to be expressed. It is necessary to use anecdotes to let history happen, to introduce a narration of beginning middle and end into it. The selection of an anecdote to narrate the significance of an occasion is more important than the general sense of what was actually said or done. As Fineman acknowledges, the anecdote may not be at odds with the general sense but, as we observe with New Historicism's use of anecdote, it is difficult to determine its relation to the general with any satisfaction. When at the beginning of *Shakespearean Negotiations* Greenblatt half-jokingly announces literature professors as 'salaried, middle-class shamans' there is actually a context being uncovered which, just as the anthropologist's place in reading a culture, needs to be scrutinised. There is some-thing shamanistic about New Historicist writing: the critic as one who is able to uncover energies within Renaissance writing not immediately apparent to the reader but whose tribal secrets of how such energies are located are not readily revealed.

At the end of *Shakespearean Negotiations* in concluding

[1] Ibid., p. 4.
[2] Joel Fineman, 'The history of the anecdote: fiction and fiction', in *The New Historicism*, op. cit., pp. 49–76.

a discussion of *The Tempest*, Greenblatt tells a story to exemplify 'the continued doubleness of Shakespeare in our culture: at once the embodiment of civilised recreation . . . and the instrument of empire'.[1] He relates an incident of the explorer Stanley in Africa in the nineteenth century. Stanley was accused by natives of practising evil magic because he was observed writing about them in a book. The natives insisted he burn the book or they would attack him. Worried about losing his notes, Stanley burns a copy of Shakespeare which resembles his notebook. Greenblatt records the episode about Stanley in a longish extract from Stanley's own published writing which makes a great rhetorical play on Stanley's regret at burning Shakespeare. But as Greenblatt points out, there is evidence to suggest that Stanley made up the part about burning Shakespeare to heighten the effect of his story. However, Greenblatt concludes:

> it doesn't matter very much if the story 'really' happened. What matters is the role Shakespeare plays in it, a role at once central and expendable – and, in some obscure way, not just expendable but exchangeable for what really matters: the writing that more directly serves power [Greenblatt having pointed out how Stanley's notebook proved invaluable in establishing the Belgian Congo]. For if at moments we can convince ourselves that Shakespeare *is* the discourse of power, we should remind ourselves that there are usually other discourses – here the notes and vocabulary and maps – that are instrumentally far more important.[2]

And we should perhaps add to this list of discourses the critical one which organises an anecdote, which may not have taken place at all, to re-iterate a point about Shakespeare and power. What I find uncanny here is that a book which begins with a mocking suggestion about the literary critic as shaman, ends with a story in which Shakespeare is used by an explorer pretending to be a shaman among willing believers convinced of his power. Within the narrative of Greenblatt's book – opening with him considering the 'magic' of Shakespeare revivifying the

[1] Op. cit., p. 161.
[2] Ibid., p. 163.

dead in Greenblatt's own voice, concluding with Greenblatt considering Shakespeare as substitute fetish for the book which the natives believed was stealing their life – this latter story also stands as a type of anecdote or fable about part of New Historicism's critical enterprise. Shakespeare is given a role in which his plays are presented circulating with other texts in a context of history which, upon analysis, discloses a relation between theatrical text and state power. Just as the importance of the Stanley anecdote was not whether it was true or not, in a sense it does not matter if the Renaissance cultural relations Greenblatt posits actually existed, because the truth of that cultural negotiation is exchangeable for the writing that more directly serves power, in this case the critical writing which establishes the critic as salaried shaman.

I do not wish to suggest that New Historians are involved in some huge subversive critical enterprise duping credulous students. This is patently not the case. New Historicist criticism, as I have mentioned, is formally reluctant to make generalised claims. Its focus, ultimately, is on a reading of a literary text, one usually familiar and accessible to readers who can test a New Historicist reading against their own experience of the text. However, its location and release of new energies within a literary text are based on discoveries of how that text negotiated its own culture. This is where it becomes important to distinguish whether New Historicism uses the cultural anecdote as necessary to focus the general sense of the culture, or whether it offers a selectively constructed view of the culture necessary to the roundness of the New Historicist's negotiation. It is a distinction which New Historicist writing avoids confronting. Clearly, Greenblatt's argument is compromised if, in the case of *King Lear*, we find the play and Harsnett's *A Declaration of Egregious Popish Impostures* are *both* texts on the margins of the culture, neither representative of the culture's central preoccupations.

Critical reservations about New Historicism are overwhelmed by the benefits it has produced in forcing us to reconsider the relations between texts, historical contexts, and the methodologies we use in both establishing and unravelling these relations. By combining a fuller investigation of a text's history with an awareness of new theoretical investigations into the structures of both culture and discourse, New Historicism has directly confronted the problem of how literature 'says something of something and says it to somebody' (to recall Geertz's formulation). By arguing that 'thick description' of some specific cultural action indicates larger and more significant features of the culture as a whole, New Historicism maintains contact with history as part of a larger narrative. History for New Historicism still meaningfully links past with present and even future while at the same time recognising that 'little histories' (accounts which emphasise the particularity of specific historical acts within a localised context) must be closely explicated.

In trying to allow for the distinctiveness of the particular historical origins of a text while not abandoning the claims for larger historical consequences, New Historicism may veer too much towards seeing history as symbolic. Literary texts can be seen acting as metaphors for features the skilled (shamanistic perhaps?) reader of the cultural text discerns and whose significances to the larger whole are suggestively indicated. There may be a restrictiveness in the range of cultural structures illuminated, but attempting to determine at least some of the cultural webs which emerged during the Renaissance and trying to discover why they were spun indicates the dynamism of cultural representation. New Historicism refuses to see texts as passive reflections of the cultural whole, but as interventions within it, fashioned by the whole but also re-fashioning the existing orders through which culture is written and understood.

The strength of new historical procedures becomes apparent when contrasted with aspects of 'revisionism' among current historical accounts of the early modern period. In reaction to more radical theoretical models, some historians have made increasing claims for the uniqueness of localised history.[1] Their techniques are not unlike 'thick description' in some respects: setting out accounts for a closely defined topic in an exhaustive manner and assembling a wealth of documentary and

---

[1] For a useful overview see Glenn Burgess, 'On revisionism: an analysis of early Stuart historiography in the 1970s and 1980s', *The Historical Journal*, 33, 3 (1990), pp. 609–27.

statistical evidence to assess an event. The difference
with New Historicism is in a refusal to see the incident
or localised concern as symbolic or as a metaphor for larger
cultural significances. Indeed one of this form of revisionism's characteristic positions is to stress localised events
happening as a result of localised pressures rather than as
responses to larger national happenings or, especially, to
articulated ideological movements. Insisting that detailed
historical evidence makes it hard to categorise and structure
a developed narrative to specific events, this revisionist
historical practice refuses to determine anything beyond
what 'the evidence' precisely articulates. The role of the
current interpreter as both reader and writer is diminished.
Indeed, the interpretive role is restricted and its ideological
claims negated through an appeal to pedantic accuracy,
pointing out that cases for larger historical significances are
almost impossible to determine. This is not to imply that
this form of historical revisionism is ideologically neutral
or objective. Its contextual critical focus frequently is to
attack those who claim to perceive cultural preoccupations which revisionism sees as ideologically disruptive to
established (and establishment) views of English cultural
development. Much recent historicist revisionism within
the early modern period has been particularly vocal in
opposing those who attempt to discover an organised
political character among those groups outside the formal
organisation of official state policy.[1] Since distinct evidence
for political actions is contained overwhelmingly in official
records, repudiating the use of other forms of cultural
documents on the grounds that they can not be clearly
interpreted becomes an implicit acceptance of the state's
officially articulated view of social, political and cultural
organisation. At an extreme, such detailed localised studies
can appear to demonstrate that during the early modern
period no one outside a state-sanctioned minority of policy
makers had, let alone acted on, an idea which had alternate
social and political implications, rather than responded to,
say, the price of corn in a specific market.

A revisionist history's emphasis on 'local knowledge'

[1] See for instance Davis, *Fear, Myth, and History*, op. cit. (Chapter 1, note 9), and
fundamentally J. S. Morrill, *The Revolt in the Provinces: Conservatives and Radicals in
the English Civil War 1630–1650* (London, Allen and Unwin, 1976).

does usefully challenge a creation of the easy narrative which balances a symbolic reading of some specified cultural documents (literary texts, material artefacts, theatrical performances) with the critical desire of re-energising the past. It may stress the past as different and difficult to know, an important corrective to those who claim to discover the past 'speaking' on the basis of only a couple of selected voices. But in its refusal to negotiate culture and politics outside of localised concerns, and its adoption of a methodology which details relations between social structures and their representations largely with a view to correct supposed imaginative misrepresentations, this form of localised history must remain only of limited interest. In particular, what much of it fails to do is to convince all but a handful of academic specialists that its closely delineated studies are anything more than detailed local knowledge, an interesting but benign academic pursuit. We may praise the detailed work and massing of information, but we may sleep.

New Historicism's interest in larger cultural issues, with a current focus on the politics of reading, does offer a possible mode for addressing history as doing more than detailing localised concerns without slipping back into some grand historical narrative constructed through unaddressed critical assumptions. At a time when the debate about what should be taught and how it should be taught is being hotly addressed in schools and higher education, new historicist procedures help confront a problem forcefully made by Raphael Samuel:

> Historical knowledge is in the end indivisible, even if the multiplication of specialisms seem to subdivide it into separate spheres. As a learning process, history is supposed to be about making connections, situating particular moments in large wholes, discovering a principle of order in the midst of seeming chaos. As a mode of explanation it involves bringing the outside in, and linking the particular to the general. Grand narrative, whether we recognise it or not, provides us with our markers of historical time and space. It is something which the learner craves even if teachers think they can do without it.[1]

[1] Raphael Samuel, 'Grand narratives', in 'History, the Nation and the Schools', *History Workshop Journal*, 30 (1990), pp. 127–8.

Samuel's argument uses the example of 'nation', which he points out historians of the left have shied away from either as a subject of study or as a symbolic category. Yet, as Samuel warns: 'even if nation is expelled from the class-room, it will still carry on an underground existence in the corridors and playground and an altogether more uninhibited one on television and the football terraces. If historians refuse to teach it, there will be plenty of others who will'.[1]

New Historicism offers a possible negotiation of the problem Samuel sees not only as pedagogically necessary but as politically necessary too. With its interest in cultural representation, the stories people tell about themselves, New Historicism is concerned to explore not only how the Renaissance fashioned itself, but how our present cultural categories allow us both to write and to understand culture. As we witnessed in the examples with which this chapter opened, cultural negotiation is not merely about amassing information but about interpretation of texts which, of necessity, are obliged to adopt constantly shifting devices (to recall the terms of Wyatt's sonnet). New Historicism opens the possibility of a critical analysis of a text which attends to its cultural substance rather than relying on reductive formulas to account for text and context. New historical practice has yet to develop the critical accountability it should possess, yet its efforts in confronting the questions of our access to history need to be encouraged.

It may often seem that some critical practitioners within established disciplinary frameworks which insist on treating literary texts as documents or, oppositely, as eternal works of art or according to a closely defined theoretical structure, proffer pronouncements on texts and history which are exclusively self-confident and definitive. These critical approaches can appear to possess a rigour New Historicism lacks. The problem of this critical practice wedded exclusively to a narrow disciplinary framework is that its rigour is based on 'reductive formulas', certainties about how the past is to be discovered and what Renaissance culture was. If New Historicism sometimes seems to fall

[1] Ibid., p. 127.

victim to certain formulas, such as subversion and containment, there are others it challenges. It is, to date, the most organised critical practice to insist that our understanding of Renaissance culture can be arrived at only through complex negotiations of both text and history.

5
Civilisation and Its Discontents: The Case of Edmund Spenser

In this chapter I want to examine how some of the ideas outlined in the last chapter can redirect explorations of some Renaissance texts. In particular, I want to consider how Spenser's *The Faerie Queene* may be seen negotiating within the context of Elizabeth's England. To do so I want to use another Spenserian text, *A View of the Present State of Ireland*, as a further means of elucidating some of Spenser's designs. Spenser's views on Ireland, exemplifying certain Elizabethan attitudes to a different impinging culture which England sought to control, also illustrates the unease experienced within English culture itself. What I want to suggest is that far from representing a glorification of a golden age, confident and stable in its social organisation, *The Faerie Queene* exemplifies a very uneasy social and cultural fabric and I want to indicate some of the reasons for that unease. Further, this chapter also sets out to exemplify some of the problems we confront in considering an undisputed literary text (*The Faerie Queene*) in the context of a piece of writing which does not purport to be a fiction (*A View of the Present State of Ireland*), yet which uses the generic and rhetorical conventions of literary writing. Does *The Faerie Queene* insist that it is to be read in such a manner that its role as *a history* (which as both epic and romance it can claim to be symbolically) must be seen as intrinsically different from the account of the English in Ireland which Spenser outlines in *A View*? Is not a separation of Spenser's literary preoccupations with *The Faerie Queene* from his political preoccupations in *A View* the result of later critical directions which disliked presenting literary texts as political – especially when the politics is of an insupportable type within current liberal democracies? Additionally, and perhaps even more uncomfortably, how does a consideration of Spenser and Ireland impinge on our understanding and involvement with the current 'Irish Problem' (an involvement which may be extremely immediate for some readers)? Or, indeed, the reverse, how does our understanding of Ireland currently impinge on our reading of Spenser?

Early in 1990, the Irish courts refused to extradite Owen Carron and two Irish Republican Army (IRA) suspects to Northern Ireland. Shortly after an IRA land mine exploded in Northern Ireland killing four members of the Ulster Defence Regiment. There was nothing to suggest the two events were linked. Neither was particularly exceptional within the catalogue of events that have taken place during the last twenty years. However, it was linked by Mrs Thatcher, who suggested that it signified that the Irish Republic was less committed than Britain in bringing the IRA to account for their crimes: 'You take these murders of these four people today alongside the decisions in the Supreme Court not to extradite those accused of violent crime – and one is very, very depressed'.[1]

Some months later a colleague and I were returning to London from a meeting in Brussels. It was clear when we arrived at Heathrow airport that security was very tight. I travel on an Irish passport and in going through Immigration was looked up in a register of, I presume, suspects. I was not listed. However, the Immigration Officer started questioning me. The questions were fairly predictable but the hostility of the tone was apparent. At this point my colleague behind me (British passport holder, immaculately dressed, well spoken) stepped up and casually pushing forward his passport said: 'Oh he's all right, teaches at London University.' 'Oh yes', replied the Immigration Officer, 'which part?' When I replied he looked at me, then at my colleague, and addressing *him*, said, 'Oh well, at any rate he was born in Canada.'

A few months later, the IRA killed the Member of Parliament, Ian Gow. Commentary at the time largely recognised that it was yet another atrocity designed to antagonise political and public sympathy and hopefully upset co-operation between London and Dublin. From predictable corners, it produced predictable calls for sterner measures and greater vigilance against terrorism. It also produced the following leader from the conservative *Daily Telegraph*:

[1] *The Guardian*, 14 February 1990.

The weak link in the struggle against the IRA continues to be the will of the Dublin government and the Irish people. Only when Dublin has the courage publicly to take action to root out the killers in its midst . . . will progress be made. As long as the Irish Republic provides a safe haven for substantial numbers of known terrorists, the British people will hold the Irish people in some measure responsible for the tragedies wrought by terrorism.[1]

Each of these anecdotes reflects a certain common facet of the English experience of Ireland – a mistrust of it. In my own relatively trivial example what struck me forcefully was the assumption that being born in Canada seemed to make me more 'one of us' in the Immigration Officer's eyes than 'one of them', despite the fact that, within terms of the European Community, being Irish should make me far more of an insider. Both the former Prime Minister's and the *Daily Telegraph*'s implications that Ireland condones the IRA, that it somehow condones terrorism, reflect the depths of mistrust which is part of the British experience of Ireland. The *Telegraph*, too, implies that British can be neatly distinguished from Irish, but one of the complexities of Britain and Ireland is that it is not that easy to do so. IRA terrorists from the North may be travelling on British passports. Are they 'us' or 'them'?

Spenser's *A View of the Present State of Ireland* was written during 1596 but because it advocated far more severe measures than Elizabeth's government would tolerate it was not allowed to be published until 1633 when it appeared in a somewhat watered down version edited by Sir James Ware. Spenser's ideas are presented in the form of a dialogue between Eudoxus ('of good report', 'honoured') and Irenius (the masculine form of Ireland). The former is the voice of sound, sensible England, the latter is Spenser who had been granted land in county Cork in 1588. Irenius is set upon convincing Eudoxus that harsh policies are necessary to subdue and civilise Ireland and that a more moderate approach, which might appear sensible from the vantage of civilised English life across the Irish sea, is inadequate to deal with the dangers posed by Ireland. Spenser's Irenius is presented as the voice of experience, the man who has front-line knowledge of the Irish and

[1] *Daily Telegraph*, 1 August 1990.

who, as the dialogue tries to show, has a firm grasp of
the Irish situation past and present. But Spenser's is also
the voice of apocalyptic concern. The Irish question for
him is part of larger questions about the maintenance of
civilisation in a hostile world.

Spenser recognises that this last perspective is unlikely
to seem immediately convincing to a supposedly rational
English audience. He, therefore, uses his rhetorical skills
to persuade the level-headed but inexperienced Eudoxus
that Irenius's fears are not unreasonable when the nature
of the Irish situation is grasped. His technique shows a
masterful grasp of the conventions of the philosophic dialogue perfected by Plato. There is an appearance of debate,
but increasingly Eudoxus asks rhetorical questions which
allow Irenius to answer at length, and (hardly surprisingly)
win Eudoxus over to see the sense of his proposals once
the true horror of the Irish are recognised. Rhetorically,
Spenser's text is organised so that it increasingly appears
that Eudoxus has no counter-arguments to put to Irenius,
such is the ostensible soundness of Irenius's evidence and
arguments. Eudoxus thus appears well-intentioned but
naive, while Irenius emerges as the source of reason and
experience. Spenser, thus, hopes to persuade his readers
that the extremity of his views is, in fact, not extreme
at all.

Irenius begins his account with an expression of anxiety
which reveals a number of linked issues which constantly
crop up in Spenser's writing: the establishment and maintenance of true religion and civilisation within a pattern of
human development predetermined by the divine. What
worries Spenser is how human action fits in with this
determined overall scheme of things whose main signposts
can be discerned in Scripture, but whose timetable and
precise unravelling are not clear. Change haunts Spenser,
even when he acknowledges that a providential order is
operating. At the tract's beginning, Eudoxus inquires how
it is with the advantages of Ireland as a place for agriculture
– a key aspect for establishing civility – that it remains
savage. Irenius responds:

> Marry, so there have been diverse good plots devised and
> wise counsels cast already about reformation of that realm,
> but they say it is the fatal destiny of that land that no

purposes whatsoever are meant for her good will prosper or take good effect, which whether it proceed from the very genius of the soil, or the influence of the stars, or that Almighty God hath not yet appointed the time of her reformation, or that He reserveth her in this unquiet state still, for some secret scourge which shall by her come unto England, it is hard to be known but yet much to be feared.[1]

Eudoxus scorns this answer, arguing that it is typical of acts with failed human agency (the 'good counsels' devised) to throw the reasons for their failure on to divine agency, 'so as to excuse their own follies and imperfections' (pp. 1–2). Spenser at this stage is establishing his own claims to rational soundness by having Eudoxus, with his common sense English perspective, be seen marginalising the apocalyptic claims of Irenius. But the rest of *A View* is formulated to transform readers' approval to Irenius without loosing Spenser's claims to be pursuing the Irish question in an impartial philosophic way.

As we see in the passage above, Spenser also establishes from the outset the sense that Irish questions participate in larger questions of reformation and the establishment of civilisation. He sets Ireland up as a type of extreme place – a place possibly cursed in its very soil or divinely reserved to act as a scourge for England. He is creating a context which will help to justify his severe proposals for treating Irish resistance to the processes of civilisation (proposals which include genocide). Severe actions may be sanctioned against Ireland because it is naturally cursed, or because it needs extreme measures to bring it the fruits of reformation (desired by God), or because it holds some particular horror for England which the English will deserve unless they do something about it. Using this last possibility, Spenser implies that the English acting firmly against Ireland might demonstrate that they have purified the fault which was going to cause Ireland to scourge them in the first place, namely a tameness in executing God's designs against savage immorality. It also indicates the much more haunting proposition for Spenser,

---

[1] Edmund Spenser, *A View of the Present State of Ireland*, W. L. Renwick (ed.) (Oxford, Clarendon Press, 1970), p. 1. All citations are to this edition.

that Ireland may scourge England because that is what is divinely desired and there is no escape. The prospect of a civilisation being overturned by an allowed evil getting control is a real fear for Spenser.

A View of the Present State of Ireland enforces its perspective of the savage nature of the Irish by giving them a curious ethnogeny. Spenser considers whether they are Scythian in origin or whether they may have originally come from Spain. The latter he rejects because it is clear the Irish are too barbarous even to be Spanish, but he supports the former account of origins. Scythians were depicted by the Greeks as being the most untamable savage barbarians. Thus, Spenser proposes that Irish savagery excels anything that could be associated with England's most apparent enemy, Spain. He further gives the Irish a notorious classical origin, making an implicit equation between the civilised English and Greeks, and the worst ancient barbarians and the Irish. If England felt the recent victory of the armada against Spain to be a confirmation of God's approval of the English as an important elected and reformed people (a view Spenser allegorically depicts in *The Faerie Queene*, Bk V, VIII), Spenser, in projecting the English as inheriting mantels of both classical and Christian supremacy, is inflating the need for subjecting Ireland to a moral conquest of epic proportions.

Spenser's fears about Ireland become most apparent, however, when he turns to the subject of the 'Old English' there. During Spenser's time Ireland was inhabited by three distinct groups. First, the native (or in Spenser's term 'mere') Irish. Second, the Old English, descendants of settlers who had come over with the first wave of English conquest during the Middle Ages. Third, the 'New English' settlers who had been given land by the Tudors in a number of plantations. Spenser was a member of this third group. What *A View of the Present State of Ireland* saves its worst condemnation for is those Old English who had 'degenerated' and gone native even to the point of abandoning their original names and taking Gaelic ones. For Spenser they become even more malicious to the English than the 'mere' Irish. Eudoxus inititally is shocked by this possibility: 'Is it possible that any should so far grow out of frame that they should in so short a space quite forget their country and their own names?' (p. 64). But Irenius provides sufficient example to bring Eudoxus to proclaim: 'In truth, this which you tell is a most shameful hearing and to be reformed with most sharp censures in so great personages to the terror of the meaner' (p. 66).

Here Spenser reveals a particular fear, the tenuous-ness of civilisation. What antagonises him is the prospect of the civiliser being rendered savage, the moral made immoral. Ireland provides distinct evidence that civilisa-tion in the hands of the few must be maintained by exclu-sivity (Irenius insists that any social contact between Eng-lish and Irish be suppressed and expressly advocates for-bidding the English the opportunity of learning Gaelic). The savage becomes a disease which can infect the civil, and the disease is best eradicated by harsh medicine. This anger and fear about Old English degeneracy was a com-mon complaint among numerous New English settlers. Politically, expressing horror at degeneracy was expedient. The Old English tended to be the most influential group within Ireland during Spenser's time. They, far more than the New English, had the ear of Elizabeth's government and they advocated restraint in dealing with Ireland. It suited the more militant and ambitious New English to portray them as having Irish sympathies and having gone native. But Spenser's fear seems more genuinely deep seated. Spenser, or the inheritors of his estate, are most at risk of catching the same savage disease. Irenius makes the point that the Old English within the actual English Pale (the area around Dublin directly ruled by England) have been preserved in reasonable civility. It is rather those in the most outlying areas of Connaught and Munster (where Spenser's estate was situated) who have grown to be 'as very patchcoks as the wild Irish' (p. 64). Where savagery is allowed to remain it is not static but works to corrupt the civilised. From *A View of the Present State of Ireland*'s perspective the civilised, the moral and the godly are equated. To allow savagery to remain is to allow evil to remain.

Having persuaded Eudoxus that Ireland must be re-formed, Irenius answers his question as to how this can be accomplished other than by laws and ordinances. It must be accomplished by the sword:

Even by the sword, for all those evils must first be cut away
with a strong hand before any good can be planted, like
as the corrupt branches and the unwholesome boughs are
first to be pruned, and the foul moss cleansed or scraped
away, before the tree can bring forth any good fruit.

(p. 95)

Spenser, however, does not literally mean the sword. One
of the difficulties he acknowledges is that the Irish are not
given to fighting 'civilised' battles on a properly organised
battle field. Rather they fight guerrilla campaigns, as befits
their savagery, which are extremely difficult to subdue.
Spenser advocates that large sections of forest on each
side of the road could be cut down to prevent ambush.
He believes, though, that a winter campaign against the
Irish is the best medicine as they will then be unable to
find sufficient replenishments and can be starved into
submission. He cites approvingly the use of this tactic
in suppressing the rebellion in Munster, noting how the
Irish were subdued through famine:

> Out of every corner of the woods and glens they came
> creeping forth upon their hands, for their legs could not
> bear them. They looked like anatomies of death, they spake
> like ghosts crying out of their graves, they did eat dead
> carrions, happy where they could find them, yea, and one
> another soon after, insomuch as the very carcasses they
> spared not to scrape out of their graves, and if they found
> a plot of water cress or shamrocks, there they flocked as to a
> feast for the time, yet not able long to continue therewithal,
> that in short space there were none almost left, and a most
> populous and plentiful country suddenly left void of man
> or beast. Yet sure in all that war there perished not many
> by the sword, but all by the extremity of famine, which
> they themselves had wrought.

(p. 104)

Spenser approves this because it does not drain English
resources through having to keep a large standing army
in Ireland. But he also likes this method because it appears
that the famine is caused by the Irish themselves as a result
of their lack of husbandry (which confirms their savagery)
and, thus, appears a natural reward of their refusal to
accept the civility of English rule.

A Present View of Ireland presents a rather disturbing
presentation of the means through which Spenser desires

to conduct his civilising mission in Ireland. In his well designed writing, too, Spenser reveals that the fruits of Renaissance humanism with its concern for eloquence (a matching of rhetoric and substance) as a demonstration of moral civilised life can be used to argue genocide. The recent debate about whether Spenser is typical of 'New English' perspectives on Ireland or more extreme than most is not particularly the point.[1] What *A Present View* forces us to do is to reconsider a traditional equation between humanism and liberalism. Seeing Renaissance writing deploying its resources to justify genocide as moral, divinely justified and 'civilising', forces us to accept that Renaissance literature's role has too frequently been accepted as unquestionably an instrument of enlightenment in some unexplored way. A student of mine in a Spenser class which read *A Present View* suggested it seemed peculiar to be reading a piece by an author commonly hailed as one of the great writers of the English Renaissance putting forward views which makes him a type of war criminal within a twentieth-century perspective. This may seem a harsh sentence, but it does highlight how literary studies often seek to purify its canon either by exclusion or, more readily, by representing uncomfortable aspects of texts in ways which reduce their conflict with twentieth-century liberal values. It might be worth recalling Walter Benjamin's view that there is always a verso and recto to history – each document of civilisation is at the same time a document of barbarism.[2] It depends who is viewing what from which perspective.

In which respects should *A Present View of Ireland* be linked with *The Faerie Queene*? The preoccupation with the establishment and maintenance of civilisation and true religion is a central feature of Spenser's poem as it is with his political tract. *The Faerie Queene*, though, ostensibly emphasises personal development: 'The generall end therefore of all the booke is to fashion a gentleman or

[1] See Nicholas Canny, 'Edmund Spenser and the development of an Anglo-Irish identity', *Yearbook of English Studies*, xiii, (1983), 1–19; Ciaran Brady, 'Spenser's Irish crisis: humanism and experience in the 1590s', *Past and Present*, III, (1986), 17–49; Nicholas Canny and Ciaran Brady 'Debate, Spenser's Irish crisis: humanism and experience in the 1590s', *Past and Present*, 13, (1988), 201–15.
[2] Walter Benjamin, 'Theses on the philosophy of History', *Illuminations*, Harry Zohn (trans.) (London, Jonathan Cape, 1970), pp. 258–9).

noble person in vertuous and gentle discipline' (p. 15). So Spenser wrote to Sir Walter Ralegh in a letter almost certainly designed to be printed with the poem. As we have seen in an earlier chapter, by gentleman or noble person Spenser is thinking of a distinctive class of person, but his desire to fashion gentlemen nevertheless might be seen as directed at individual development. Criticism of the poem has usually stressed this individual moral cultivation. As Stephen Greenblatt noted some years ago, though, for a poem devoted to gentle discipline there is a great deal of violence.[1] Certainly, attempts to read the poem at a wholly symbolic level with the violence being explained away as allegorical representations of abstract moral conflicts ignore the great deal of interest the poem shows in history, particularly Spenser's contemporary history.

Spenser is not interested in history from some disinterested secular perspective. Rather the events he symbolically depicts are part of a larger design to reveal a *historia*, an unfolding of a pattern which is to be found both in the self and in a social and political fabric. Spenser uses the commonplace theory of correspondences not merely as a convenient poetic device, but to reflect his belief in linkages and parallels among (from our perspective) apparently diverse ideas. Belief in the microcosm reflecting the macrocosm and vice versa does not produce some bland reflection of a theory of stable order. Rather correspondences between micro and macro produces greater fears about disruptions and instabilities. Loss of control in the self (particularly the 'selves' of powerful individuals), or loss of control in a wider social or political fabric could produce a domino effect bringing the whole into chaos. Being concerned with gentlemen or noble persons, in other words those within the society who were in a position to act, Spenser directs his poem to make them aware both of dangers and responsibilities.

Spenser's preoccupation is characteristic of a Renaissance humanism which believed literature could move right readers to moral purpose. But such humanism did not see morality as a passive condition. Virtue was manifested by acting virtuously, not through passive reflection.

---

[1] Greenblatt, *Renaissance Self-Fashioning*, op. cit., esp pp. 173–7 (see Chapter 4 note 7).

Humanism considered the most powerful or most noble within society to be the best readers and directed writing at them not exclusively because writers looked to this class for generous rewards or for some snobbish appeal. The powerful could act, they were the ones with the scope to control and change active social conditions. They were potentially the best readers because they could act upon their reading. The idea of reading *The Faerie Queene* in an armchair and then announcing oneself as having gained virtue was a largely foreign concept to Spenser's brand of humanism. For Spenser, the poem's effect, in essence its success, should be measured by how its designs were acted on. The virtuous person participated in virtuous actions within the social fabric. Without such actions any claims to virtue were hollow.

Spenser's ideas of moral reform, therefore, cannot be divorced from ideas of political and social reform within actual contemporary situations. Not surprisingly *The Faerie Queene* shows how individual conduct and wider political conduct are closely linked. These correspondences help provide the clues to the often disparate nature of the poem's various episodes. Structurally, there often appears to be a type of miscellany within each book of *The Faerie Queene*, with a loose narrative organisation bringing the disparate episodes together into some inconclusive whole. What the structure tries to provoke, though, is an awareness that the maintenance of self-control is the means by which the wider social and ultimately religious fabric is controlled. The self and the society cannot be separated.

I want to examine how some of Spenser's concerns are manifested in *The Faerie Queene* through an examination of Book V. The book is concerned with Sir Artegall or Justice. It is the part of the poem which is most fundamentally centred on Ireland, as Artegall's principal quest is to free Eirena from her enslavement by Grantorto, a cruel giant. The request for release from monstrous tyranny is made by Eirena herself to the Faerie Queene, whose champion Artegall is. If Irenius in *A Present View* was a masculine version of Ireland, Eirena is a feminine personification (though both, of course, are English prescriptions of what Ireland *should* be). The quest to free Ireland begins Book V and the successful slaying of Grantorto is in the final canto. The basic conceptual structure is clear. Ireland is presented as a place whose feminine nature makes the country require a more powerful masculine presence to keep it from the savagery of the giant who is unmistakably a Roman Catholic monster. There is a potential civilised nature to Ireland, and it is this side which asks English help. The opposition, which must be suppressed, is savage Roman Catholicism encouraged by the giant.

As with all the books of the poem, however, Artegall's quest is immediately interrupted by other events, apparent deviations and distractions from his task. Most diverting is Artegall's encounter with the Amazon Radigund whose sexual allurements cause him to be captured and emasculated by being dressed in woman's clothes and forced to spin. He is freed by Britomart, his betrothed, whose chastity gives her great military powers. The episodes with the Amazons occupy the centre of the book, but rather than being unconnected with Artegall's Irish quest, they are linked. Spenser throughout the book, and indeed throughout the poem, makes a number of equations which sit at the centre of his ideology. Right rule is ordered, self-controlled, Protestant and masculine. Wrong rule is disorderly, uncontrolled, Catholic, and feminine. Spenser's world is not black and white, there are mixtures of these various combinations, but what is apparent is that a deviation from the right mixture invites disaster. Thus Eirena or Belgae (the Netherlands) in Book V are shown to be ladies of virtue but vulnerable to aggression from Roman Catholic masculine tyrants. Artegall himself is rendered helpless when he loses self-control through Radigund's allurements, allowing not only himself to be debased but the continuance of a disorderly Amazonian government. Even Britomart, who seems at times Spenser's ideal, is presented as open to uncontrollable fury because of her feminine nature. It is interesting to contrast Britomart's fight with Radigund with Artegall's final contest with Grantorto. Both are held under chivalric conventions of a formal confrontation between champions. But the women's fight immediately loses control and Spenser depicts them as a tiger and a lioness, beasts confronting one another with animal fury unnaturally seeking to attack their legitimate feminine identity:

> With greedy rage, and with their faulchins smot;
> Ne either sought the others strokes to shun,
> but through great fury both their skill forgot,
> And practicke vse in armes: ne spared not
> Their dainty parts, which nature had created
> So faire and tender, without staine or spot,
> For other uses, then they them translated;
> Which they now hackt & hewd, as if such use they hated,
>   (V, VII, 29)

Britomart wins because her rage is greater. Even in victory, however, Britomart does not immediately regain composure she: 'Stayd not, till she came to her selfe againe' (V, VII, 34) but for a mixture of motives – revenge, anger, pain from her wounds – she decapitates Radigund. Thus in the women's fight, Spenser presents the two combatants not as fundamentally different but very similar. Britomart's superiority appears later when she recognises the right order of things and restores masculine rule, freeing Artegall and the country: 'And changing all that forme of commone weale,/The liberty of women did repeale,/Which they had long vsurpt; and them restoring/To mens subiection, did true Iustice deale' (V, VII, 42).

In contrast, Artegall's final encounter with Grantorto, again organised as a formal chivalric contest, shows Artegall as intensely self-composed and controlled as opposed to the giant's enraged but chaotic behaviour. Artegall fights as a skilful mariner controls his vessel in a storm (V, XII, 18) and defeats the giant by carefully watching for the right advantage. Spenser depicts Artegall also beheading his opponent in victory, but almost compassionately: 'He lightly reft his head, to ease him of his paine' (V, XII, 23). Thus, by the end of the book, Artegall has come to learn self-control which ensures his victory over uncontrolled savagery. His victory over the giant is the result of skill and control not fury as was the case with Britomart's victory. Both Britomart and Radigund forgot their skill in battle (whether they also forgot their feminine nature or revealed it is more difficult to determine). Artegall keeps control and this allows victory over a savage force which appears much larger and more powerful than the knight.

This emphasis on the triumph of masculine order is the

context of Book V's final cantos. When Artegall was captured by Radigund, his squire and assistant, the iron man Talus – who flails the lesser rabble and common criminals with unemotional, unsparing, but Spenser emphasises, just punishments – had to seek the means to free his master. At the book's end, with the triumph of controlled, masculine, Protestant order, Talus becomes the effective instrument of his master. Spenser depicts Artegall's rescue of Eirena as a triumph and return of civilisation to Ireland. Artegall remains with her for a time and restores order:

> His studie was true Iustice how to deale,
> And day and night employ'd his busie paine
> How to reforme that ragged common-weale:
> And that same yron man which could reueale
> All hidden crimes, through all that realme he sent,
> To search out those, that vsd to rob and steale,
> Or did rebell gainst lawfull gouernment;
> On whom he did inflict most grieuous punishment.
>
> (V, XII, 26)

This should be the culmination of Artegall's task. But Spenser has Artegall forced to return to the Faerie Court. He is vague about the precise reason, suggesting merely 'He through occasion called was away' (V, XII, 27) but he links the recall with how Envy (a feminine personae) spreads malicious rumours about Artegall because of his victories in Ireland which were against her desire. Thus Artegall's 'course of Iustice he was forst to stay,/And Talus to reuoke from the right way' (V, XII, 27). This episode bears considerable similarity to the fate of Lord Grey de Wilton, Lord Deputy of Ireland to whom Spenser acted as secretary. Grey was recalled because the Old English persuaded Elizabeth that the severity of Grey's tactics in repressing Irish rebellion were counter-productive. Spenser obviously approved of Grey's measures.

Spenser's depictions in Book V are more than just an attempt to justify Grey. Artegall's subduing of Ireland is a conclusion to acts of masculine orderly restoration which the book as a whole deals with. After the return of right masculine rule from the tyranny of the Amazons, Artegall meets with Prince Arthur and the two of them accomplish various overthrowing of tyrannies. Arthur restores liberty and right religion to Belgae. What Spenser presents then is a process by which a militant English chivalry reforms a Europe beset by Roman Catholic tyranny and savagery. Ireland is the last and potentially most significant episode here – at least structurally it is the concluding adventure. Its 'restoration' seems to promise much, but the promise is interrupted by Artegall's being required to return to the Faerie Queene's court. Artegall's initiative in Ireland is not completed and savagery is allowed to regain a hold. The failure to conclude Ireland's 'restoration' to civility is also a failure of the processes of defeating the forces of savagery throughout northern Europe, which is what the book as a whole has been symbolically accomplishing. Although Spenser does not make it explicit, this failure occurs not because of further disruptive forces from outside confronting Artegall but through his recall to the court of the Faerie Queene. The cause of Artegall's inability to subdue Ireland in a completely satisfactory way is the result of actions proceeding from the civilised centre, not from those of the Faerie Queene's opponents. The book concludes with Artegall subject to the taunts and slanders of the hideous hags Envy and Detraction. Artegall will not confront them or allow Talus to flail them, and the book ends not with Artegall's triumph but his return to Faerie Court with these two ugly figures taunting him.

The savage in Book V is closely equated with the uncontrolled, and noticeably with Roman Catholic tyranny. The ravaging giant of Eirena's territory finds counterparts in other figures depicted as monstrous, cruel, degenerate, and corrupt. Their relation to the Beast of the Apocalypse and other figures of Satanic inspiration are often apparent. But what is also clear is that ideal figures such as Artegall are also susceptible to being undone, particularly by feminine guile. Spenser's world is not filled with unassailable knights, even his heroes are open to corruption. As Book V's conclusion makes clear, even Justice in his moment of apparent triumph is susceptible to unexpected interference. The forces of civilisation need to remain constantly vigilant.

The precariousness of civilisation haunts *The Faerie Queene* as it does *A Present View of Ireland*. In both texts what is particularly worrying is how the ostensibly noble can be undone. In the *View of Ireland* it is the Old English beyond the Pale, at the end of *Faerie Queene* Book V, it is the spectacle of the feminine Envy and Detraction pursuing Artegall into the realm of the Faerie Queene. In another telling episode from *The Faerie Queene*, Spenser reveals how the savage in Ireland becomes equated with the uncontrolled aspects of the individual. Book II, canto IX of the poem is the well-known house of Alma or Temperance episode. Sir Guyon (Temperance) and Prince Arthur come upon a solitary well-defended castle. Riding up they are warned away because the castle is under siege by a savage horde, but almost immediately they are set upon:

> A thousand villeins round about them swarmed
> Out of the rockes and caues adioyning nye
> Vile caytiue wretches, ragged, rude, deformd,
> All threatning death, all in straunge manner armd
> Some with vnweldy clubs, some with long speares,
> Some rusty kniues, some staues in fire warmd.
> Sterne was their looke, like wild amazed steares
> Staring with hollow eyes, and stiff vpstanding heares.
>
> (II, IX, 13)

This is remarkably similar to Irenius's descriptions of Irish dress and manners recounted in *A View*, details designed to demonstrate the savagery of the Irish. Not only does Irenius decry the Irish appearance, making the bestial comparisons Spenser also proposes in the above passage, he also dwells on their uncivilised forms of fighting such as attacking suddenly with hit-and-run tactics. In this episode from *The Faerie Queene*, Spenser makes the Irish connection explicit. These villeins (meaning the attackers are peasants, not gentlemen, and thus are not socially entitled to attack knights) are compared to insects which rise out of Irish bogs:

> As when a swarme of Gnats at euentide
> Out of the fennes of Allan do arise,
> Their murmuring small trompets sounden wide,
> Whiles in the aire their clustring army flies,
> That as a cloud doth seeme to dim the skies;
> Ne man nor beast may rest or take repast
> For their sharpe wounds, and noyous iniuries,
>
> (II, IX, 16)

The military skills and superior armaments of the two knights allow them to fight off their attackers and they gain admittance to the castle. Spenser makes it clear that the villeins are not individually dangerous to the superior knights. Rather, like insects, they are annoyances except when they seem to possess such overwhelming numbers. What he does do, though, is present these foes as mysterious and indefinably threatening in a haunting manner: 'For though they bodies seeme, yet substance from them fades' (II, IX, 15).

Gaining access to the castle, the knights are given a tour. The castle is a human body and while retaining a conventional castle architecture, Spenser sets out to show how the well-organised body is a fortress which can maintain itself from attack by savage exterior forces. As numerous commentators have pointed out, the 'castle' appears to share many of the same physical features as Spenser himself. At the end of the tour the knights are shown three of the chambers of the mind: phantasy, judgement, and memory. Spenser dwells longest on the first, revealing it filled with 'infinite shapes of things dispersed thin' (II, IX, 50). What is interesting is that the insect imagery used to characterise the villeins is continued here. Phantasy's chamber:

> filled was with flyes,
> Which buzzed all about, and made such sound,
> That they encombred all mens eares and eyes,
> Like many swarmes of Bees assembled round,
> After their hiues with honny do abound:
> All those were idle thoughts and fantasies,
> Deuices, dreames, opinions unsound,
> Shewes, visions, sooth-sayes, and prophesies;
> And all that fained is, as leasings, tales, and lies.
>
> (II, IX, 51)

Properly controlled, phantasy is obviously an important part of a poet's castle, when by profession he is a 'maker', a fictionaliser in some sense. But what Spenser demonstrates is that uncontrolled phantasy lies close to the destructive savagery which lurks, similarly insubstantial and 'dispersed thin' without. The maintenance of the castle is more than a concerted defence of the ordered interior against the disorderly exterior. The interior, too, contains elements which are potentially destructive. As the experience of most of his knights throughout the poem reveals, they contain within themselves the opposite of their virtue and only through ordered self-control can they turn their powers to good. But, as Spenser's discussion of the Old English going native in *A View of the Present State of Ireland* reveals, the destructive interior elements when placed in an environment where their exterior corresponding elements are present may gain possession of a potentially good individual or group and bring about degeneracy. The well-tempered individual's ability to maintain order is precarious when he is located in a terrain which is uncontrolled. The savage, debased, and bestial presences which attack virtue, may undermine its integrity because the potential to degenerate into villainy lies within even a nobleman. It is precisely because of this danger that extreme measures are needed to suppress the savage.

As we see, therefore, for Spenser in both poem and tract there are explicit parallels. The establishment of order and civilisation in Ireland (according to an English model) is required because only in such a context can nobility, proper religion, and morality prosper. Without the cultural context conducive to virtue, baseness, Roman Catholicism, and immorality become menacing realities even for the both spiritually and militarily fortified minority of civilised individuals. But, while it should be apparent now how this strikes anxieties within Spenser's specific Irish context on the supposed margins of civilisation, it also indicates more fundamental anxieties about the Elizabethan world in general.

Spenser wrote *A View of the Present State of Ireland* not as a vindication of Elizabethan policy towards Ireland but as a document highly critical of it under a necessarily respectful guise. For Spenser, Elizabeth and her ministers are the Eudoxus of the piece – good intentioned but lacking the knowing attitude toward Ireland which Irenius possesses. Spenser's design was to change Elizabethan policy, to have Lord Grey and others of the New English who advocated severely repressive measures recognised as acting in the best interests of civilisation, social order, and true religion. As indicated, Spenser was unsuccessful, his tract censored. Similarly, *The Faerie Queene*, while apparently lauding

Elizabeth, actually seems severely uncomfortable with her. As we have seen, the feminine is at some fundamental level uncontrollable within the poem, even Britomart succumbs to passions which cause her knightly skills to lapse. At Book V's conclusion, Artegall is a knight returning to the civilised centre accompanied by two feminine personifications of vice. The knight may hold 'his right course' (XII, 43) but Envy and Detraction remain a hostile destructive force at the civilised centre as well as the savage margin. At the end of Book VI, Spenser has the offspring of these vices, The Blatant Beast, roaming the world and doing the poet harm by spreading slanders, again at the supposed civilised centre of the courtly world. In certain respects this disruption within the civilised centre results from the controlled masculine Artegall being unable to finish his work in subduing the savage margins in Eirena's kingdom. The reason for this failure seems ultimately to lie with the ideology of The Faerie Queene herself.

Like many others during his age, Spenser developed a variety of tactics to try to fudge the fact that England was ruled by a woman. This meant transforming Elizabeth into a type of divine principal whose sexuality was not directly addressed.[1] Each book of *The Faerie Queene* approaches Elizabeth under oblique but obvious disguises as a para- gon, yet each book reveals anxieties about women and fears about their potential duplicity. Women sometimes are virtuous, while at other times they only appear so in order to lure men to destruction. But Spenser also makes it clear that it is difficult and sometimes impossible to distinguish between the true and the false, regard- less of how clear-sighted and self-controlled his masculine knights may be. As David Norbrook has shown, the Faerie Queene had another guise in sixteenth-century England as a mischievous black-faced trickster, who at least some peasant rebels claimed to be led by.[2] Further, even when the virtue of a feminine personae is not questioned (as in the case of Belgae or Eirena), the rule of a woman is shown to be insufficient to combat the irreligious evil

---

[1] Phillipa Berry, *Of Chastity and Power: Elizabethan Literature and the Unmarried Queen* (London, Routledge, 1989).
[2] David Norbrook, *Poetry and Politics in the English Renaissance* (London, Routledge and Kegan Paul, 1984) pp. 109–56.

which had gained control of their land. In the first book of *The Faerie Queene*, Una, another paragon of virtue, is shown needing a male champion to defeat the Roman Catholic Satanic dragon which is destroying her parents' kingdom. She may be virtuous, but she is not capable of defending civilisation against its attackers.

The position of Spenser's Elizabethan gentleman is revealed to be a precarious one. The court of the Faerie Queene from where the knights are dispatched is absent from the poem. There appears no civilised pale where they can remove their armour and let down their guard for any length of time. The virtues the knights seek to develop, both in themselves and in the world, are always under assault. Just as the individual's own make up (as revealed in the House of Alma episode in II, IX) is shown to contain elements which are potentially destructive, so it is implied that the civilised centre from which the knights supposedly originate is not impervious to the savage. Significantly, that centre is not even readily discernible. The implication is that it is readily observable in the reality of Elizabeth's court, but Spenser keeps the relation between Faerie Queene and Elizabeth ambiguous. Prince Arthur's quest for the Faerie Queen which is found throughout the poem is never concluded. Spenser suggests that the marriage and the subjection to masculine virtue, which the success of this quest would entail, would be a triumph. But Arthur's success remains as elusive as the court of the Faerie Queene.

In both *A View of the Present State of Ireland* and *The Faerie Queene* Spenser reveals his anxieties about the resilience of the savage, the apparent inability of England to deal effectively with it. What both texts indicate is that one explanation of this state of affairs may be a failure of resolve on the English side, an internal lethargy. Interestingly, in Book VI of *The Faerie Queene* Sir Calidore, or Courtesy, abandons his quest for the Blatant Beast to experience a pastoral idyll. England's failure may be traced to irresolution at the society's centre, the Queen herself. It is Artegall's required attendance at the Faerie Court which prevents him from completing the renewal of justice in Eirena's kingdom, and it is Elizabeth, *A View of the Present State of Ireland* makes clear, who halted the

necessary civilising action undertaken by the New English
there:

> Her Sacred Majesty, being by nature full of mercy and
> clemency, who is most inclinable to such pitiful complaints
> and will not endure to hear such tragedies made of her
> people and poor subjects, as some about her may insinuate,
> then she perhaps for very compassion of such calamities
> will not only stop the stream of such violence and return
> to her wonted mildness, but also con them little thanks
> which have been the authors and counsellors of such
> bloody platforms.

(pp. 105–6)

Under the guise of complimenting Elizabeth's mercy,
Spenser is implying she is easily manipulated by others.
Her nature (a just monarch or a sentimental female?) makes
her clement – but the text is clear that this form of clemency
is not desirable and suppresses the perpetrators of justice
not its opponents. The apparent failure of the English to
contain the Irish reveals a great deal of weakness about
the English in Spenser's eyes.

Patricia Coughlan has argued that *A View of the Present
State of Ireland* is the founding text of modern English discourse about Ireland.[1] Spenser certainly found ready contemporary imitators, most noticeably among fellow poets
such as Barnabe Rich or Sir John Davies whose interest in
Irish affairs also provoked them to write political tracts.[2]
These provide evidence that, if Spenser's tract was not
published before 1633, it obviously circulated in manuscript. But in a much wider sense it is also noticeable,
in reconsidering the examples of present Anglo-Irish relations with which this chapter opened, how there exist
apparent similarities between at least some current English
discourses about Ireland and Spenser's. The Irish as a
people are still imagined as involved, at least tactily, in
perpetuating a contemporary form of savagery – terrorism. Ireland is still witnessed as a state in some indefinable way opposed to England. Certainly, among extreme

---

[1] Patricia Coughlan, ' "Cheap and common animals": the English anatomy of Ireland in
the seventeenth century', in *Literature and the English Civil War*, op. cit., pp. 205–26
(see Chapter 1, note 4).
[2] For example see the texts assembled in James P. Myers, Jr (ed.), *Elizabethan Ireland:
A Selection of Writings by Elizabethan Writers on Ireland* (Hamden, Conn., Archon
Books, 1983).

Ulster unionists we continue to find a discourse of anti-Catholicism which employs scriptural apocalyptic images which one suspects would be more readily comprehensible to late sixteenth- or seventeenth-century audiences than they are to most twentieth-century ones. But it is not only extremist rhetoric from Ulster sects which entails a view that British troubles with the IRA are part of some wider battle between civilisation and savagery. Responding to Ian Gow's death, his widow declared: 'Eventually right will always triumph. The ultimate battle has already been won'.[1]

It is interesting to ask whether the qualities Spenser conferred on the Irish, making them the hostile out-siders who needed to be suppressed but who his texts acknowledge to be also a lurking part of the civilised English, are still part of current English imaginative experience. English hostility and mistrust of the Irish cover uncertainties and insecurities about the position of civilisation and savagery on both sides of the Irish sea. Equations which Spenser made between religion, class, morality, and self-control (especially in sexual matters) as a register of civility or savagery, and ultimately of good or evil, may be found uncannily, certainly uncomfortably, circulating within our current social discourses.

In a recent interview with *The Spectator* Lord Denning, former Master of the Rolls – one of the highest judicial positions in England – commented that he felt the Guildford Four and the Birmingham Six should have been hung because everyone would then have forgotten about them.[2] The Guildford Four and the Birmingham Six were con-victed of separate incidents of bombing pubs frequented by soldiers in the early 1970s as part of an IRA campaign. The Guildford Four were freed in 1990 after it became clear that evidence used against them had been fabricated by the police. At the time of the interview, I rather discounted it. Lord Denning is 91 and not really to be held responsible for views arising from senility. However, I changed my mind about the seriousness of Denning's pronouncements when it was declared a few weeks later that the case of the Birmingham Six was to be reconsidered. It now appears

1 *Daily Telegraph*, 1 August, 1990.
2 *The Spectator*, 17 August 1990, pp. 8–10.

evidence was fabricated in their case, too, and in 1991 they, too, were released. When still practising, Lord Denning had refused to allow an appeal against their conviction. Granting such an appeal he felt would have endangered respect for the law. It would, it seems to be implied, have suggested that the forces of civilisation (the British police and legal system) were capable of acting as savages, seeking to punish people guilty only through shared racial origins in order to maintain the appearance of control and order which civilised societies require. 'We shouldn't have all these campaigns to get the Birmingham Six released, if they'd been hanged. They'd have been forgotten and *the whole community* would be satisfied' (my emphasis).

What Lord Denning's *Spectator* interview in his dotage had revealed was unguarded language. The principles out of which his remarks had arisen were the same as when he held high office. A key element in both the Guildford and Birmingham prosecutions at the time of the original trials were confessions from the accused. These confessions were withdrawn by the accused because they claimed they were extracted from them under duress, including beatings. The police claimed the confessions were genuine and no coercion had been used. The police were believed. The integrity of judicial and other institutions which enforce justice rely on their being perceived as impartial in their administration. Behind Lord Denning's concern to protect these institutions' reputation was the fear that they would be discovered to be other than how they try to protect themselves, and that their integrity would be compromised. The maintenance of appearances, even if it required a suppression of state violence and a tacit blind-eye to the imprisonment of the innocent, was paramount. It is interesting that Lord Denning in concluding his interview chose the dying words of John of Gaunt from Shakespeare's *Richard II* to foretell the decline of Britain into what he believes is a 'tenement' of Europe. Maintenance of English civilisation is upheld by keeping exclusive English control.

Here, it seems, we have a current example of Britain needing to conceive of savagery belonging to outsiders, not a part of British civilisation but an external force which could undermine British institutions unless repressed. In the need to maintain a belief in civilisation, practices are condoned which, in this case, allowed the Irish to be guilty by racial association for atrocities carried out by members of the IRA. Maintaining the appearance of the civilised centre fighting the savage margins (and Europe is still a margin for some) displaces any confrontation of potential savagery at the centre, and the anxieties that raises.

Yet, there also appear dangers in resting content with proposing apparent similarities between past and present and leaving them on the table, as it were. This is not to discount their existence. But to imply, in however tentative a way, that there have not been some fundamental changes in the English experience of Ireland since Spenser's day, helps on the one hand to re-energise the Renaissance texts by demonstrating their continuing cultural negotiations, but also curiously helps to valorise Spenser's perspective. One of the criticism's frequently directed at anthropological methods of inquiry is that they cause cultures to be presented as being essentially static. The underlying cultural patterns anthropologists seek means the implications offered by changing historical circumstances are given insufficient attention. At its most dangerous this can allow unsavoury political or social practices to be 'forgiven' because they are presented as stemming from some cultural constant within a society. Clifford Geertz's analysis of Balinese culture discussed in the last chapter, for example, has the unfortunate appearance of explaining the extremity of anti-communist violence which took place on the island in the mid-1960s as somehow linked to something essential about the Balinese as a society.[1]

My model in reading Spenser is based on assumptions that these texts act as types of cultural registers, they provide indications about how Elizabethan society charac-terised itself. As should be clear, this does not mean that Spenser was 'a typical Elizabethan' (if such a creature can ever be said to exist). As we see, his texts were to reform English actions not celebrate them. Spenser is arguing from the specific perspective of a militant

---

[1] Geertz 'Deep play', op. cit., see note 43, p. 37 (see Chapter 4, note 15), see also Vincent P. Pecora, 'The limits of local knowledge', *The New Historicism*, op. cit., pp. 243–76 (see Preface, note 3).

Protestant New English settler in Ireland and that hardly makes him a typical Elizabethan. What I am suggesting is that Spenser's texts offer glimpses of issues which Elizabethan culture found awkward to confront directly – a belief in the precariousness of its civilisation given the existence of savagery (exemplified by other customs, baser classes, other religions) confronting a self-defined orderly minority. Further, Spenser helps us to discern cultural issues which Elizabethan institutions prevented being openly represented, notably the uneasiness generated by a woman ruling within a patriarchal culture.

These issues continue to lurk in social experience today, but they do so in profoundly different ways. English mistrust of Ireland, even though the rhetoric between 1600 and 1990 seems similar, is based on different conceptions from Spenser's time. The whole question of nationalism is of a very different order. It may suit some English commentators to think of the IRA as only a terrorist force rather than the Irish Republican Army because the acronym represents the IRA as shadowy forces of savagery and evil, which by definition it is difficult for the civilised good to understand. But the IRA characterise themselves in a more discernible form, participating in movements of national liberation from colonialist powers in recognisable patterns of nineteenth- and twentieth-century political experience. Like many other minority organisations, we can refute their legitimacy in adopting this guise. But approaching the IRA from a nationalist perspective is very different from seeing them as savage, without apparent objectives other than the spread of evil. One of the dangers then in making a link between Spenser and certain current perspectives is that it suggests that Spenser's view of England and Ireland is a founding dicourse which iterates a cultural conflict intrinsic to English experience. What is more important, is the realisation that, while Spenser's discourses, both *Faerie Queene* and *A View*, are energised by their immediacy to pressing cultural concerns, these discourses themselves energise later perspectives. The power invested in Spenser's literary representations helped establish patterns which became culturally entrenched even to the point of resisting changing historical categories.

Spenser represented real cultural preoccupations in his texts but these representational forms became vehicles which helped enforce cultural categories and the apparent identities they confer. Spenser was the most important English influence on English literary writing throughout the seventeenth century (just as Milton was throughout the eighteenth). In large numbers of writers (many now seldom encountered) we confront replications of designs, language, and generic adoptions which recall Spenser. This is not, of course, to imply Spenser is some form of original fountainhead of these echoes and similarities many of which are encountered throughout Renaissance culture. But Spenser's particular deployment of many widespread literary and wider cultural features had a notable impact on English writing during the following century. Subsequent writers re-orient and transform Spenser's devices to different contexts. What results, though, is not a nebulous diffusion of Spenserian energies, but their reinforcement. Spenser's iterations that England and Ireland were representative of a key conflict in an unfolding revelation of good and evil become familiarly established with readers who find Spenser's terms repeated in similar patterns in other texts and different contexts. Spenser's texts increase their expressive power within subsequent literary cultures, finding their own power increases by being reflected in later texts which have channelled these Spenserian texts for their own uses.

Examining Spenser and Ireland, therefore, raises more questions about relations between literary texts and historical contexts than it resolves. Easy categorisation about the literary and the historical are rendered impossible. The importance of a literary text as a representation of Elizabethan culture is clear, but defining and characterising its status as representation is not. It may misrepresent English and Irish experience to draw analogies between Spenser and current perspectives, but it equally is misplaced to deny that past and present discourses about Ireland possess noticeable similarities which have larger cultural consequences. The relations between what may be termed the aesthetics of cultural generatio

6
The Drama's Place

I The State of Play

Christopher Marlowe's play *Doctor Faustus* has long perplexed students of the Renaissance. One of the central problems confronting any discussion of a text for the play is which version should be used. There are two main versions, a text published in 1604 (commonly known as the A text) and another published in 1616 (the B text) which is half as long again as the A version. There are, additionally, seven other quarto editions of the play published between 1604 and 1631, all with minor variations on one or other of the two main versions, as well as records which indicate there was a 1601 quarto which is not now extant. Marlowe died in 1593. We know *Doctor Faustus* was acted in 1594 and throughout the 1590s. It was almost certainly acted in 1589. The conditions of its composition and even a precise date for the play are uncertain.[1]

There is nothing particularly unusual about *Doctor Faustus*'s early stage and printing history, except for the number of editions. It is always useful to recall that while we celebrate Elizabethan and Jacobean drama as a literary highlight of the English Renaissance, the drama was not readily perceived as serious literature by the majority of those who watched plays or even by the minority who bought the plays in cheap unbound quarto editions. John Donne may have been a great frequenter of plays, but the catalogue of his books he produced in the early seventeenth century reveals no dramatist among the many contemporary English writers he assembled.[2] Printing plays in a cheap, unbound, quarto format indicates that the drama was commonly perceived as on the same

[1] The fullest discussion remains W. W. Greg (ed.), *Marlowe's Doctor Faustus 1604–1616: Parallel Texts* (Oxford, Clarendon Press, 1950); for a more recent discussion see David Ormerod and Christopher Wortham (eds), *Christopher Marlowe; Dr Faustus: the A-Text* (Nedlands, University of Western Australia Press, 1985).
[2] See Gerald Eades Bentley, *The Profession of Dramatist in Shakespeare's Time* (Princeton, Princeton University Press, 1971), pp. 50–1.

standing as almanacs, joke books, pamphlets, and other popular writing which appeared in the same form. Thomas Bodley, the founder of Oxford's Bodleian Library, worked extremely hard in the opening years of the seventeenth century to gather books for his institution. He persuaded the Stationer's Company that they should send him a copy of each book its members printed. Yet Bodley was unhappy about including plays and other forms of cheap popular literature, feeling such texts devalued the library. Writing to the Bodleian's first Librarian, Thomas James, in 1612 he contrasted English drama unfavourably with the learned drama of other countries:

> For they [plays of other nations] are most esteemed for learning the languages, and many of them compiled by men of great fame for wisdom and learning, which is seldom or never seen among us. Were it so again, that some little profit might be reaped . . . out of some of our playbooks, the benefit thereof will nothing near countervail the harm that the scandal will bring unto the library, when it shall be given out, that we stuff it full of baggage books.[1]

Bodley's view about the literary insignificance of English drama was formally challenged by Ben Jonson who published plays in the Folio edition of his *Workes* in 1616 and later, and in response to Jonson's success, by Shakespeare's first editors, Heminge and Condell, who brought out the First Folio of Shakespeare's plays in 1623 (eight years after Shakespeare died). Including plays in the expensive and handsomely produced folio format announced the works as worthy of serious reading by serious readers. But elevating the status of contemporary drama to 'works' published in a folio edition was extremely unusual in the period before 1642 when the plays were actually being performed.

The popularity of the drama as a genre which participated in English or, more accurately, within London life of the period in ways other than as literary texts has become critically more significant during the past decade with the increased emphasis on literature's cultural contexts. Even the works of a poet such as Spenser, highly acclaimed by

[1] Ibid., pp. 52–3.

many other contemporary writers and influential on them, were only available to be read by a very few. Spenser's work was published in small and costly editions. This was in keeping with the desires of poets such as Spenser to have their work accepted seriously by high culture and who, thus, sought conditions of production which would ensure they addressed an exclusive audience. As Milton was later to recognise, fit Renaissance readers were also likely to be few. Inevitably, these readers' representative quality within larger Renaissance social discourse was partial and limited. Ben Jonson actually takes delight in announcing (in Latin) on the title page of his 1616 *Workes* that the book is designed for the select few and not the common crowd.

A folio edition was an expensive item, but even cheaper quarto editions of most writers were not available readily. There was no system of book distribution in any modern sense (and of course no effective postal service). In London, and to a lesser extent in Oxford and Cambridge, readers could find some recent English literary publications with little effort, but it was only a minority who had the inclination or resources to do so. Milton's *Poems 1645* which includes works such as *Lycidas* took over twenty years to sell out its first edition, which, at best, was something of the order of 1500 copies and more likely to have been much less, probably a few hundred. The first edition of *Paradise Lost* was printed in an edition of around 1300 for which Milton received £5. This was doing reasonably well by seventeenth-century standards for recent literature.[1]

In contrast, a play could be performed to thousands at a time. The drama was popular with the complete social spectrum. Very ordinary people (or at least ordinary men) could afford to attend a performance of a Shakespeare play in the large Globe Theatre, and appear to have done so, and the same play might be requested to be performed at court.[2] There were also many critical voices raised against 'playing', again from across a wide social spectrum among those who considered dramatic performances idolatrous or who were concerned that plays sowed social disorder. If

[1] Parker, *Milton*, op. cit., p. 601; H. S. Bennett, *English Books and Readers 1603 to 1640* (Cambridge, Cambridge University Press, 1970), p. 227.
[2] Andrew Gurr, *Playgoing in Shakespeare's London* (Cambridge, Cambridge University Press, 1987), esp. pp. 59–71.

the drama was not considered literature by many, it was the cultural form which engaged a much more significant proportion of English Renaissance society than any other form of secular writing.

This chapter seeks to explore some of the implications of drama as a popular form, distinguished in terms of its place and material existence from other literary writing within the English Renaissance. The drama poses some challenging questions to modern interpreters precisely because of its difference. The plays have been a focus not only of critical activity employing new models for interpretive inquiry but also of scholarly activity which has contested many previous assumptions about how plays were performed, codified into texts, and circulated within society.

One of the most fundamental questions which has been posed is whether we can properly speak about the drama as writing. Certainly, there were texts of some plays printed and obviously plays were originally written in some sense. Indeed, the conditions of Elizabethan and later Stuart regulation of drama required a written text. Initially, The Master of the Revels who licensed plays required the players to appear in person and present the play before his official. By 1590, however, the number of new plays was such that this was no longer practicable and companies of players were required instead to submit manuscripts before the play was acted.[1] The licensing of the play-text rather than the performance conferred a form of authority on the written artefact and it was this that was supposedly acted.

There were, though, no organised mechanisms to ensure that the play performed was the play written. There are numerous records of actions being taken against plays which were considered slanderous to nobles or which were perceived to be in political opposition to government policy, such as Middleton's *cause célèbre*, *A Game of Chess*, which opposed James's accommodating attitude towards Spain and attracted the protest of the Spanish ambassador. But, if there were some actions of censorship against plays which had been able to secure licences, it is also true that neither Elizabeth nor the Stuarts possessed the developed

[1] Bentley, *The Profession of Dramatist*, op. cit., pp. 149–50.

civil service or police force which could regulate every performance. In the majority of cases the plays did not formally raise specific political concerns which would warrant such close regulation. Plays were constantly revived and while the Master of the Revels might be expected to relicense a revival, this did not frequently happen. Shakespeare's *The Winter's Tale*, for example, was revived in 1623 more than a decade after its first appearance. The King's company apparently had lost the original licensed manuscript but the Master of the Revels was prepared to accept the word of the company manager John Heminge (one of the First Folio's editors) that 'there was nothing profane added or reformed'.[1] This does not mean that the play was not performed with alterations. Heminge may merely have been indicating that *The Winter's Tale* was unlikely to prove controversial to a censor in whatever version it was performed. Our earliest play-text of *The Winter's Tale* is that of the First Folio, also of 1623, and whether this represents a play-text from the missing licensed text or a later version we do not know. The companies of players did not perceive their plays as fixed texts, literary works which they felt some obligation to present accurately. This is not to suggest the players did not take the plays they performed seriously or that authors wrote any old thing as long as it pleased. If Shakespeare showed little inclination to control the condition of his plays' textual printing, he was both a part owner of the company which produced them and was himself a director of that company. Artistic control was paramount in terms of the production, the medium through which the play was overwhelmingly disseminated among contemporary audiences.

What this condition of the theatre indicates is that the establishing of a singular text for many plays is extremely difficult. It is not only a question of there being a number of versions for popular plays, such as *Doctor Faustus*, which were revived over a forty- or fifty-year period resulting in corrupted, revised, or differing texts. The whole question of whether we should imagine the plays as fixed in textual form is a pressing consideration. Yet, literary criticism,

---

[1] Ibid., pp. 158–9.

past as well as present, desires a fixed text. Questions of authorial intention or even authorial ascription may no longer be paramount within critical inquiry, but discussing texts as cultural documents implies that there is a discernible document, an artefact. The nature of that artefact, its meanings and position within the culture may be open to debate, but the assumption is that the document is there to be deciphered. Can this properly be said to be the case with a play such as *Doctor Faustus*?

For many years scholars have tried to establish either the A or B text of the play as more authoritative. As indicated, the later B version of the play is half as long again as the A text. Does this mean that the A text is a cut text? Or does it mean that the longer B text is an entirely different *Doctor Faustus*? There have been book-length studies devoted to trying to resolve the question of *Doctor Faustus*'s text. Much energy has been devoted to trying to establish which version is more likely to have been Christopher Marlowe's. As Michel Foucault reminds us, though:

> aspects of an individual which we designate as making him an author are only a projection, in more or less psychologising terms, of the operations that we force texts to undergo, the connections that we make, the traits that we establish as pertinent, the continuities that we recognise, or the exclusions that we practice.[1]

Establishing an authorial version of the play is usually an editorial attempt to give that version authority over others. Creating the authored version allows us to talk of corrupted texts, using a vocabulary with resonances of healthy and diseased versions. But with Renaissance drama, where performed versions were those in widest circulation, the question of the authority of a reputed authorial version is at best confused. To some extent it is fair to ask who is the play's author: the writer, the company or the director producing the play, or perhaps most properly a collaboration between these three? With Renaissance drama it is more accurate to talk of numerous plays called *Doctor Faustus* or *King Lear* or *Hamlet*, a number of differing versions circulating at almost identical times.

[1] Michel Foucault, 'What is an author?' Josue V. Harai (trans.), in David Lodge (ed.) *Modern Criticism and Theory: A Reader* (London, Longman, 1988), p. 203.

We can gain some inkling of this through our own conditions of theatre-going. Over the past twenty years I have seen about a dozen performances of *Hamlet*, a play which was also constantly revived in the early seventeenth century. With some exceptions the performances during the 1970s were constructed around the psychology of Hamlet, in the 1980s on the political context of the Danish court in which Hamlet was the most significant but by no means only player. I have seen one production which used the 1603 quarto version, one which used the uncut Folio text, but the majority were 'constructed' texts, omitting different passages and scenes from what is a very long play. From witnessing multiple performances of *Hamlet*, I would find it impossible to speak about a singular, authoritative version of the play. But, of course, the performed *Hamlet* is not the medium through which my thinking about the play has largely been derived. Rather a text of the play is my principal experience of it, in the case of the scholarly Arden edition complete with a daunting textual apparatus which can be examined at leisure. Thus, I speak even of my theatrical experience in terms of reference to printed texts – witnessing a quarto *Hamlet* or the uncut Folio text. For the majority of those who experience *Hamlet* today the play's textual medium is paramount as the point of reference to what *Hamlet* may be. With increasingly elaborate explorations being conducted into the establishing of texts, editors, even when acknowledging alternate readings, present impressive scholarly authority for creating an authorised version – the text on the page around which the variants and explanatory comments exist as supplemental scholia. During the Renaissance, and especially in Shakespeare's case before the First Folio, such textual authority did not exist. To imagine a single *Hamlet* in terms of contemporary Renaissance experience is misleading.

There is much to dispute in Foucault's scepticism about the author when applied to authored texts in circumstances where the authorial presence is clear. We should distinguish between Ben Jonson's desire to confirm his authority over his *Workes* – collecting and seeing texts through the press, attempting to control what was ascribed to him and how these texts were to be viewed, even trying to restrict his readership – and circumstances where such authorial interventions are absent. Foucault's remarks are sustained, however, when we come to attempts to author *Doctor Faustus*. Here desires to construct a version of the play that best reflects Christopher Marlowe is decidedly the result of continuities and exclusions recognised (and desired) by editors anxious to contain the play, to create a singular text where more than one exists.

Most students' experience of *Doctor Faustus* is of the longer B text, though often with an apology from editors who prefer the shorter A version on aesthetic grounds.[1] This preference is apparent when examining most critical discussions of *Faustus* – the major additions to the play found in the B text are substantially ignored. Jonathan Dollimore has noted that 'one problem in particular has exercised critics of *Dr Faustus*: its structure, inherited from the morality form, apparently negates what the play experientially affirms – the heroic aspiration of "Renaissance man"'.[2] Dollimore perceives that critical opinion has tried to resolve this issue by tending to read the play as either vindicating Faustus or the morality structure. Dollimore himself sees this conflict and contradiction as part of the play's design, 'not an affirmation of Divine Law, or conversely of Renaissance Man, but an exploration of subversion through transgression'.[3] For Dollimore, whose reading of the play in *Radical Tragedy* has been one of the more persuasive recent accounts, Faustus is the site of a power struggle between God and Lucifer, both equally responsible for his destruction. The play, therefore, interrogates heavenly power as much as hellish power and finds them both tyrannical – clearly upsetting any recourse to the older morality tradition as a satisfactory explanation for Faustus's demise. Rather, transgressing the norms of the morality tradition, Dollimore perceives the play demystifying the limiting structures of Faustus's world, without presenting the opportunity for escape. For Dollimore, therefore, *Doctor Faustus* becomes 'an important precursor of the

[1] For example J. B. Steane (ed.), *Christopher Marlowe: The Complete Plays* (Harmondsworthy, Penguin, 1969), pp. 261–2. Steane's text of Marlowe's plays is the one I cite from.
[2] Jonathan Dollimore, *Radical Tragedy: Religion, Ideology and Power in the Drama of Shakespeare and His Contemporaries* (Brighton, Harvester, 1984), p. 109.
[3] Ibid.

malcontented protagonist of Jacobean tragedy'.[1] In these later plays the limiting structures become socio-political ones, a result, possibly, of censorship which hindered the drama confronting religious issues directly.

The tensions between structure and substance noted by Dollimore and earlier critics are most apparent in the A version of the play. Here the structure of the older morality tradition is most neatly challenged by images which question its norms. The implications of what we are presented with are left more dramatically open, challenging more directly the containment implied by the morality tradition. Take for example the play's conclusion in the A version. Faustus is asked by a group of fellow scholars to summon Helen as the most beautiful woman of antiquity. He does so and the company is struck by her beauty. An old man then reproaches Faustus for selling his soul and counsels repentance which Faustus inclines towards. Mephostophilis condemns Faustus for disobedience to Lucifer. Helen is resummoned and Marlowe devotes some of the play's most arousing lines to Faustus's celebration of her (V, ii, 97–116). At the same time, the old man reappears and is tormented by devils who he scorns. The play then moves on to Faustus's last scene as he awaits the elapse of his twenty-four-year contract in a fit of anxiety and apprehension. The play concludes with Faustus's offer to burn his books and his cry/invocation/cursing of Mephostophilis. A stage direction suggests devils appear and Faustus goes off with Mephostophilis. But, even if we accept these directions as a legitimate part of the A text, what Faustus's damnation consists of is not clear. The chorus finally appears to offer a chilling exegesis of how we should regard Faustus's hellish fate:

> Whose fiendful fortune may exhort the wise
> Only to wonder at unlawful things,
> Whose deepness doth entice such forward wits,
> To practise more than heavenly power permits.
>
> (V, iii, 24–7)

The scene between the old man and Helen sets up precisely the type of orthodox structure and subverting spirit Dollimore indicates. Intellectually, the appeal is to

[1] Ibid., p. 119.

a morality structure which contrasts Christian asceticism with Satanic debauchery. Aesthetically, both verbally and visually, the scene belongs to Helen. If Hell consists of such illusions, is it so awful? Of course, those who argue in favour of the morality tradition being decisive in the play point to Helen being a succubus and an insubstantial hellish projection. Possibly, but the A version does not really confirm or deny this, or provide any clear resolution to the play. This irresolution confronts the norms by which the morality structure seeks to contain the play. By not confirming the structure, the structure's limits are revealed and the possibility of constructing the world differently, though not particularly heroically, arises.

The B version of the play is much less accommodating to this perspective. Consider the additions to the play's end. Immediately after the scene with the Old Man and Helen, Lucifer, Beelzebub and Mephostophilis appear to consider Faustus's 'lunacy' in thinking he can 'overreach the devil' (V, ii, 11–20). There is a scene in which the good and bad angels appear to reveal (from above) the throne of celestial happiness and (from below) 'the vast perpetual torture-house' of hell (V, ii, 109–42). Faustus's fate is also made clearer by the addition of a scene before the final chorus where the scholars come to visit him on the morning after his final hour and find his body torn in pieces (V, iii, 1–19). It is possible to argue these additions to the ending still leave a degree of irresolution between substance and structure open. They certainly help to enhance a perspective that sees Faustus as a pawn between two more powerful forces. But it is also clear the later text is stressing the morality tradition of Faustus. The end of the B version depicts hell and heaven in far more conventional terms, allowing these conventional limits to dominate the parameters in which Faustus's actions may be interpreted.

It is probable that neither version of *Doctor Faustus* represents the play as originally written by Marlowe. This is not because it can be proved one way or the other that either or neither version is the type of play that Marlowe would have written. Both versions reveal similarities with Marlowe's other work, but Marlowe's other work is also eclectic and difficult to categorise. This question of an editorially constructed author is one which challenges our preconceptions of a fixed writer in charge of a manuscript the integrity of which was zealously guarded. Dramatists during the period frequently collaborated on their work and the dramatists were also close to the companies producing their plays. Plays evolved, sometimes through the author's own changes, sometimes through changes in the conditions of playing. But distinguishing why changes take place is problematic before we have the evidence, as in Jonson's case, of an author wishing to impose authority on to a text. The case of *Doctor Faustus* exemplifies how we cannot be sure which version of the play was the more common experience of audiences and whether they understood the two versions as offering something markedly different or not. It could be the case that version A was perceived as a radically sceptical play and that the B version later came to dominate because the authorities were unhappy with the other version which more manifestly challenged orthodoxies. It could be that the play's audiences were more content with a version which conformed more readily with recognised long-repeated models for understanding the world, and thus preferred the longer B version of *Faustus*. It is possible both versions may have circulated as productions in Marlowe's own time, as well as in the later 1590s and throughout the early seventeenth century. The evidence to confirm a host of spculations on whether we have one, two, or more plays called *Doctor Faustus* is not readily available.

The difficulties in authorising one version of a play which has a multiple existence has been a preoccupation of Shakespearean editors over the last decade. The debates have been particularly focused on *King Lear*. The recent Oxford University Press Shakespeare publishes two versions of the play, one the 1608 Quarto *Lear* and another based on the 1623 Folio version.[1] Shakespearean editors are showing considerable innovation in moving away from the view that Shakespeare had a fixed conception for his plays, where variants between texts are 'error of transmission', corruptions which crept in because Shakespeare was not

---

[1] Stanley Wells and Gary Taylor (eds), *The Complete Oxford Shakespeare* (Oxford, Oxford University Press, 1987).

involved in preparing his plays for print. However, in terms of considering the impact of recent theoretical directions most editors are still very conservative. What they will now allow is that Shakespeare revised his plays. The 1608 *Lear* is published by the Oxford editors because they feel it sufficiently different from the Folio version to justify seeing it as a separate aesthetic entity. The Folio *Lear*, however, is believed to represent Shakespeare's final intentions. It is permitted to speak of multiple versions, but editorial principles are still seeking to create authorised versions, this time based on a 'final' revision. Revision is assumed to be a teleological operation, the process of an autonomous author in control of an autonomous aesthetic entity. The Oxford editors, no less than earlier editors, amass textual and bibliographical hypotheses to argue forms of dramatic and aesthetic evolution. Several previous generations of editors presented a picture of Shakespeare's evolving genius based on complete plays jumping out of his head in a pattern of development that made those appearing in the seventeenth century 'more mature' than those appearing in the sixteenth. The current generation of editors prefers to see this maturity exemplified in the 'final versions' produced during Shakespeare's later years. The new editorial policy complicates the process of producing authorised versions, but it does not substantially change it. The editor now pursues 'variations in composition' with a view to unlocking final intentions. This may leave open the possibility of conflicting 'final' with 'best' intentions, but in practice it is unlikely to. The editorial authorised final version is likely to be presented as the best (most mature, fullest) version.

As we witnessed with *Julius Caesar* in considering canons in Chapter three, ostensibly objective scholarship reflects many unvoiced assumptions on the part of the editor. As Foucault and others have argued, the construction and then privileging of the author as a text's origins is a product of editorial desire, matched with assumptions that establishing origins is a way of clarifying a text's destination.[1] Even recent editorial work on Shakespeare

---

[1] See Foucault, 'What is an author?', op. cit.; Roland Barthes, 'The death of the author', in *Image-Music-Text*, Stephen Heath (trans.) (London, Fontana, 1977), pp. 142–8.

foregrounds the plays as literary artefacts in the modern sense. Editors use inquiry into a play's process of composition and of transmission to discern a conscious literary producer writing texts. But such a view of Shakespeare only emerges from the publication of the Folio, a volume, unlike Ben Jonson's, which Shakespeare took no active part in preparing. Editors, therefore, elide the problem posed by Shakespearean plays being generated during a period when their textual status was secondary to their performed status. If we can determine 'origins' in Shakespearean drama, it is likely to be through examining what evidence we can of the plays' 'destinations', the conditions of performance in the theatre matched with the cultural and social conditions of production.

Considering the two versions of *King Lear*, Andrew Gurr discusses the implications posed by the two endings of the play.[1] The Quarto version assigns the play's final lines – 'The weight of this sad time we must obey;/Speak what we feel, not what we ought to say./ The oldest hath borne most; we that are young/ Shall never see so much nor live so long' (V, iii, 322–6) – to Albany, the Folio gives the lines to Edgar. Interpretive cases can be made for both versions as appropriate and in keeping with the plays' directions. Albany has tried to do what Lear disastrously did, divide the kingdom, this time between Kent (who declines) and Edgar. If Edgar speaks the last words, they appear a sort of reproof to Albany while Edgar assumes authority over the hopes of the future. If Albany speaks, it suggests an attempt to reassert authority he has just been trying to give away (as Gurr proposes about as upbeat a close as leaving Denmark in Fortinbras's control). 'The alternate endings are about as different as they could be', Gurr concludes, 'yet all Shakespeare changed was a speech heading'.[2]

Critical study is not particularly well geared to deal with this type of problem. Students preparing for exams, as well as professional academics subtly re-interpreting texts, rely on some consensus about what texts are actually being considered. Current editorial practice elides the implications of multiple texts. We may allow multiple versions,

---

[1] Andrew Gurr, 'The once and future King Lears', *Bulletin of the Society for Renaissance Studies*, 2, 1, (1984), pp. 7–19.
[2] Ibid., p. 17.

but as long as editors are concerned to establish some idea of final versions differentiated from earlier versions, and both conceived as the product of a revising author, the question of textual authority is open to be resolved. The editor comes to assume the responsibility for choice or creation of a text. In terms of Renaissance drama this has enormous implications for trying to argue the drama as a representative cultural form. Only when the plays enter stabilising textual form do they become available for the type of sophisticated analysis critics undertake. In Shakespeare's case, only as plays moved out their popular medium of production to quarto, and finally inscribed in the Folio, do the plays become textually established in 'final versions' used to undertake theoretically complex investigation. A type of paradox is created. Current theoretical inquiry is often concerned with considering the drama within terms of cultural production, but analysis is dependent on representing the plays in a stable textual form that obscures the condition of the drama's cultural production.

There has been much important work in the past decade demystifying the editorial practice of scholarship, revealing the ideological or other cultural desires editors assume.[1] Surprisingly, though, there have been few attempts to acknowledge the fluidity of Renaissance plays. Critical discussions may emphasise the drama's popularity within English Renaissance society and examine the conditions of theatrical playing within Elizabethan and Jacobean society, but considerations of plays rarely acknowledge that many possess multiple forms. The multiplication of textual versions is likely to indicate even more produced versions. As we see with *King Lear*, a small change in a speech heading can have significant implications for interpretation. In *Doctor Faustus* whether heaven and hell are 'discovered' in a manner which confirms conventional expectations of them can have drastic implications for the play's destination, the impact it makes on its audience. As we become ever increasingly careful in our reading of texts, we need also to question what representational

[1] See for instance Margreta de Grazia, 'The Essential Shakespeare' op. cit. (see Chapter 3, note 8).

status the text has. The state of the play we read – often a composite version constructed by a modern editor – may be a necessary feature of study, but it should not hide the fact that the playing of Renaissance drama was performed in circumstances where the cultural place of the play was very different to that of the present.

II   The Politics of Comedy

Much of the *Doctor Faustus*'s expansion in the B version consists of elaborations of the play's comic scenes. Far more than the differences in the impact of the moral resolution in the various versions of the play, the scenes of low comic farce the play engages with have perplexed critical commentary. Indeed the apparent difficulties in reconciling the comic and the tragic in *Faustus* are so formidable that many critical discussions tactfully ignore any detailed consideration of these scenes. Jonathan Dollimore's account in *Radical Tragedy*, for instance, effectively ignores the farcical side to *Doctor Faustus*. Considerations of the serious conflict between hellish and heavenly power dominates most current accounts of the play. Yet the comic scenes also have a transgressive function within the texts. They parody the ostensibly serious action, creating a compromising context to the apparently more lofty power struggles. For example, immediately following Faustus's recitation of the terms by which he will give his soul to Lucifer we have a scene in which his servant Wagner engages a serving man who, Wagner announces, is hungry enough to give his soul to the devil for a shoulder of raw mutton. To this the man replies: 'Not so neither. I had need to have it well roasted, and good sauce to it, if I pay so dear, I can tell you' (I, iv, 11–12). In another scene, expanded in the B version, two ostlers (attendants on horses at an inn) get hold of some of Faustus's books. They see the benefits of magic as enabling them to get free drink and sex with the kitchen maid, Nan Spit. They conjure Mephostophilis who, for their presumption, announces that he will turn them into an ape and a dog. Their reactions are not of terror but of pleasure:

> Robin. How into an ape? That's brave! I'll have fine sport with the boys. I'll get nuts and apples enow.

Rafe. And I must be a dog.
Robin. I'faith thy head will never be out of the potage
pot.

(III, iv, 18–19)

In one of the serious exchanges of the play Mephostophilis
announces he is in continual torment because he has lost
the sight of God. Faustus (who has not had the experience)
chides Mephostophilis to learn 'manly fortitude' from him
(I, iii, 74–86). This challenges the experience of both the
hellish and the heavenly for humanity estranged from the
conditions that maintain both states – either the direct
experience of God or awareness of God's absence. This
estrangement helps emphasise Faustus caught between
two contending powers only intent on the damage they can
inflict on one another. But with the comic scenes, heavenly
and hellish power is even more directly confronted by the
debased condition of the 'clowns' (as Marlowe entitles
these servants). For them becoming beasts or selling their
souls will provide them with nourishment. They have
nothing to lose and much to gain. Their basic human
needs confront the threat posed by the satanic in the plays.
The diabolic is ridiculed through having hell's agents
summoned by clowns whose punishment for meddling
in the higher arts of magic is greeted as a reward. Satanic
punishment geared to a reduction of higher beings to
bestiality is revealed as not properly applicable to varying
human conditions, where people imagine themselves, in
the case of the ostlers, below the levels of beasts they are
employed to serve. The hierarchies of heaven and hell are
challenged not in Faustus's heoric rhetoric of confounding
hell in Elysium but in the debasement and consequent
ridiculing of supernatural power by the base condition of
the 'clowns'.

The comic scenes expose the play's serious endeavours. These scenes not only parody Faustus's activities
(for instance he, too, desires sex – his first request to
Mephostophilis is for a wife, and his last request is to
see Helen again), but also involve Faustus who engages
in comic pranks. If Faustus imagines that he will become
the master of great power, he actually uses Mephostophilis
to engage in a series of revels and to become the obliging
conjurer for the emperor and his fellow scholars. Certainly

power with Faustus does not corrupt in any conventional way and his activities remain curiously adolescent throughout. The B version, with its extended accounts of antics, reinforces a view of selling the soul as a means of engaging in revelry rather than evil.

Peter Burke in his study *Popular Culture in Early Modern Europe* has noted how dramatic players were sometimes thought of as being in league with the devil who was considered a great master of illusion.[1] Throughout *Doctor Faustus* we have Mephostophilis and even Lucifer engaging in theatrical spectacle to keep Faustus from recanting. The long presentation of the seven deadly sins at the play's centre is a form of dramatic interlude for Faustus, yet a key scene in the devil's politics of spectacle. Here we have a play performed for Faustus, but one which is a carnival-like performance, parodying sin and reducing it to low comic status. Within a morality structure this could be construed as a warning on the nature of playing itself. Faustus loses his soul to engage in theatrical playing for twenty-four years. But the comic parody within the play transgresses the morality structure, showing its limitation. The clowns, seeing Mephostophilis's curse as a benefit, travesties conventionally conceived hellish curses.

As the influential theorist Mikhail Bakhtin argued, such parodic reversals reveal a different and contradictory reality from the lofty one prompted by serious literary genres such as tragedy.[2] *Doctor Faustus* as a performed play parodies the more serious playing for souls which organised religion promoted in the real world outside the theatre. A world where the satanic was often considered a real force, either supernaturally intervening in the natural world through witchcraft or, as was more pronounced in England, working through his Roman Catholic agents. This position helped establish popular equations between hellish power and groups both within English society (Roman Catholic

---

[1] Peter Burke, *Popular Culture in Early Modren Europe* (London, Maurice Temple Smith, 1978), p. 94.

[2] Bakhtin's work is most easily approached through his *Rabelais and His World*, Helene Iswolsky (trans.) (Cambridge, Mass., MIT Press, 1968); *The Dialogic Imagination*, Michael Holsquit and Caryl Emerson (trans.) (Austin, University of Texas Press, 1981) esp. pp. 41–83. For application of Bakhtin to early modern England see Michael D. Bristol, *Carnival and Theater: Plebeian Culture and The Structure of Authority in Renaissance England* (London, Methuen, 1985).

recusants) and nations outside (the Catholic states of southern Europe). In parodying the satanic, the play challenges the myths and categories which structured that reality, laughing at the contest for souls by reducing it to theatrical revelry. This parodic function can be witnessed as a confrontation to the serious claims of social institutions outside the theatre.

As witnessed in examining Spenser in the previous chapter, an equation was made between maintaining civilised, religious government and confronting Roman Catholic savagery in real political actions. English institutions were predicated on the position that the monarch and government acted to maintain divine will. The claim to divine right by Stuart monarchs, for instance, was one of the sources of anger that led to the English Civil War, but not because the claim was widely rejected. Rather, Charles I, in particular, was accused of acting against God's interest when above all men he should be ruling according to divine norms (for Charles's critics the divine was indisputably Calvinist in organisation). This caused Charles, in some of his critics' eyes, to appear a traitor of almost satanic proportions. He, above all other humans should not have erred. Because of the monarch's greater proximity to the divine, the monarch's transgression was potentially greater than any other human being. Within this cultural framework then, a travestying of the serious powers of both hell and heaven through the laughter generated by the clowns, helps undermine the lofty claims of government to be acting in defence of civilisation.

The B version of *Doctor Faustus*, with its expanded comic scenes, is particularly engaged with transgressing conventional high cultural categories through laughter. Recall that the B version added a scene at the play's conclusion where the students discover Faustus's dismembered limbs. Within the context of the serious parts of the play, this scene seemed to confirm the unpleasantness of Faustus's damnation. But throughout the play, dismemberment of limbs has been used in comic scenes as theatrical trickery. In one instance Faustus allows his leg to be pulled off by an angry horse-trader Faustus has conned. The trader thinking he has killed Faustus, runs off, and Faustus keeps the man's money. In another scene, which is part of an elaborate exchange with a knight about the wearing of horns (a badge by which the knight reveals himself a cuckold), Faustus's head is apparently cut off. In both cases the dismemberment of leg and head are magician's tricks. In one respect it might be argued that Faustus's dismemberment at the play's conclusion is to contrast the reality of this fate against the foolery of the previous scenes. At the end of the final chorus, however, the 'restored' Faustus reappears to accept the audience's congratulations for his performance.

The nature of the theatrical performance itself parodies the serious business of saving and damning souls which is the province of religion. The use of the play-within-the play convention in *Faustus* confuses the limits between 'reality' and theatricality, the serious and the mocking. Engaging in playing is the principal activity undertaken within the play, both formally in the presentation of the seven deadly sins, but also in the construction of spectacles by Faustus and Mephostophilis of both a lofty (e.g. the presentation of Alexander to the Emperor) or farcical (e.g. the conning of the horse dealer) type. When the play concludes and the actor playing Faustus reappears whole for his applause, has the play actually stopped, or does the play indicate a similar theatricality being performed in the world that lies outside the formal bounds of the theatre?

The 'comic' scenes, then, parody the serious theatrical illusions within the play, but they also serve to dissolve the differences between comic and serious. It become impossible to categorise whether individual scenes, such as the presentation of the seven deadly sins, or the play in general is serious or farcical, tragical or comic. These parodic elements cause *Doctor Faustus* to transgress the limits of conventionally imagined heavenly or hellish power by mocking heaven's or hell's ability to control those creatures ostensibly subject to them, travestying the theatricality of heaven's or hell's power. It also mocks the realm of the learned and academic, showing the pursuits of Faustus as sharing similarities with the pursuits of the clowns. The play refuses to allow an easy separation of its parodic from its serious representations, its addressing of lofty issues and its mimicry of them. As such even the tragic genre the play's chorus tries to establish for the action is subverted through exposing the theatrical revelry which all the players engage in.

The implications of a popular culture which questioned and inverted social, political and cultural hierarchies has been a powerful influence on current Renaissance studies. The principal impetus to this critical direction has been Mikhail Bakhtin and his work on the carnivalesque. Although writing much earlier in this century, Bakhtin's work only gradually gained respect in English studies after the translation of his *Rabelais and his World* in 1968. Bakhtin is interested in the way the popular culture of 'the world from below' inverts the categories and conditions of high culture through festive misrule, the world turned upside down of the carnival where the ordinary world is parodied through forms of grotesque representation. Particularly important for Bakhtin was the importance given to exaggerations of the body. The corporeal body, and particularly its coarser functions, were used to parody activities high culture tries to present on an abstract plane. For example in *Doctor Faustus*, the sin of Gluttony gives himself an ancestry that includes a gammon of bacon for his grandfather and Peter Pickle-herring and Margery March-beer for godparents. This parodying of abstract qualities by reducing them to some form of grotesque material representation which could be laughed at was seen by Bakhtin as attacking the supposed unity of social and cultural hierarchies. The carnival decentred fixed authority, allowing for other possibilities, and revealing that established authority and its organisational categories are relative. This is true not only of the claims of political and social hierarchies, it is true, too, for the linguistic (and literary) categories which tried to structure the world exclusively.

In Cervantes' *Don Quixote* (the first part of which appeared in 1605), Sancho Panza tells a story to Quixote at one point. The story infuriates Quixote because it does not conform to the models of story-telling he expects. He tries to force Panza, who knows the story according to the terms of popular oral culture, to tell it differently. Sancho Panza refuses, 'In my country . . . all the old stories are told in this manner; neither can I tell it in any other; nor is it civil in your worship, to desire I should change the custom'.[1] The story ends abruptly when Quixote fails to take account of the number of goats transported in a boat, an incident utterly trivial according to the norms of Quixote's literary experience but crucial to the conditions of Panza's oral tradition.

For Bakhtin, such examples represent instances of what he calls the novelisation of language. Readers become aware of contending discourses, each categorising and ordering the world differently. Our awareness of this multiplicity of different voices forces a recognition of varying ways in which 'reality' can be linguistically constructed and generically represented. We come to recognise a partiality of perspective in which the claims of high and low, cultured and popular, formal eloquence and dialect slang clash with each other creating a plurality of voices, without any dominant, monologic language able to assert control. In contrast genres such as epic or tragedy insist on a common social and moral language with one dominant concept of reality. A hegemony of ideology and cultural expression is established in such genres which will not admit challenge.

Don Quixote is a parody of the chivalric tradition established through the romance genre. But in Quixote's mad attempts to pursue a world he has constructed through reading, Cervantes reveals Quixote's difference from the rest of the world is only his determination to textualise the world in an exclusive way. Other figures, from both high and low culture, within the novel are involved with the same process of attempting to live according to a constructed reality. The reason they are considered sane and Quixote mad is that their textualisation is more widely recognised and socially allowed. Sanity or madness is not determined because the ostensibly sane construct a cultural identity in some intrinsically different way from Quixote. In revealing this unfixed, comic view of the world, Bakhtin argued, texts such as *Don Quixote* or Rabelais's *Gargantua and Pantagruel* began to challenge the monological control of serious literary genres. The decentred, comic view of the world they articulated, the heterogeneous combinations of

[1] Miguel de Cervantes, *Don Quixote de la Mancha*, Tobias Smollett (trans.) (London, Andre Deutsch, 1986), pp. 141. See Roger Chartier, 'Texts, printing, readings', in *The New Cultural History*, op. cit., pp. 154–75.

styles they possess challenged any attempt to create a fixed, unitary world view.

The concepts which Bakhtin explored in Renaissance prose are also to be found in English Renaissance drama. Both forms help exemplify a wider cultural phenomena noted by Peter Burke, the re-figuring of the relations between high and popular culture during the period.[1] Burke argues that until the seventeenth century there was largely a two-way traffic between high and low culture, what Burke calls the great tradition and the little tradition. However, during the seventeenth century the upper classes gradually withdrew from the little tradition. It continued to survive, of course, but it could now be distinguished as 'popular' and its norms no longer impinged on the great tradition. Recall how in my opening chapter I noted how Milton's *Samson Agonistes*, by adopting the high cultural tragic genre, became distanced from *pp 18?* the radical popular voices Milton had some ideological sympathy with, but which he became stylistically, and thus culturally, divorced from. *Samson Agonistes* remained largely silent among those groups it might have sympathetically addressed. As we have seen above, during the early seventeenth century there were initial attempts to change the status of English drama into that of the exclusive great tradition of high culture. Jonson's *Workes* signalled on its title page that it was not seeking popular approval. Additionally, Jonson did not publish his play *Bartholomew Fair* in his Folio, a play which most particularly represents the carnivalesque plurality of voices a Bakhtinian analysis would witness as a challenge to official culture.[2] The title page to Jonson's *Workes* is illustrated with images which link Jonson with the classical theatre of antiquity (the great tradition). With the arrival of the author as a controlling factor on the plays' printed representation, the drama's links with its popular, little tradition, origins are begun to be suppressed. Indeed, Burke sees the rise of literacy generally undermining traditional popular culture.[3]

[1] Burke, *Popular Culture*, op. cit., esp. pp. 22–64; D. R. Woolf, ' "The common voice": history, folklore and oral tradition in early modern England', *Past and Present*, 120, (1986), pp. 26–52.
[2] See Stallybrass and White, *The Poetics and Politics of Transgression*, op. cit., pp. 27–29 (see Chapter 4, note 10).
[3] Burke, *Popular Culture*, op. cit., p. 16.

English drama during the Renaissance, therefore, was in the process of transforming its status, how it conceived and perceived itself, and how it was experienced. The separation between high and popular culture had not become fully established and, more particularly, many dramatists were readily familiar with the norms of both high and low culture. Just as prose writers such as Cervantes and Rabelais were interested in more confidently structuring the parodic voices of popular culture to contend directly with the serious and stylistically unitary voice of high culture, so the dramatists, confident with both grand and little traditions, confronted literary hierarchies.

A good example is immediately offered by one of the most memorable comic moments of Shakespeare's *A Midsummer Night's Dream* where Bottom the weaver appears with the head of an ass and Titania, the Queen of the Fairies, immediately falls in love with him. Bottom deserted by his companions sings a simple ditty which contains colloquial double entendres on sexual cuckoldry. He breaks off the song to analyse it with some proverbial wisdom. The singing and his remarks confirm his recourse as a 'rude mechanical' to popular song and 'market-place' wisdom as his cultural discourse. Bottom concludes his song:

> The finch, the sparrow, and the lark,
>   The plain-song cuckoo gray,
> Whose note full many a man doth mark,
>   And dares not answer nay –
> for indeed, who would set his wit to so foolish a bird?
> Who would give a bird the lie, though he cry, 'cuckoo'
>   never so?
>
> (III, i, 119–24)

In singing, Bottom has awakened Titania. Enchanted she perceives his song not as a low culture product with smutty commentary but high eloquence. She mistakes his discourse, just as much as she fails to see the ass's head makes Bottom physically grotesque. Her reaction to his shape and his song parodies the relation between eloquence and object promoted by high cultural humanism by having her address a culturally refined discourse to a wholly inappropriate subject. Speaking correctly was one of the means by which social position was established and 'worth' observed. But, as Shakespeare displays, such perceptions are based on recognitions of what is eloquent and beautiful, and human perceptions are variable and possibly deluded:

> I pray thee, gentle mortal, sing again:
> Mine ear is much enamour'd of thy note;
> So is mine eye enthralled to thy shape;
> And they fair virtue's force perforce doth move me
> On the first view to say, to swear, I love thee.

(III, i, 125–9)

Because of Titania's position, she requires her fairy servants to recognise Bottom as *she* perceives him. Her power and position coerce them to recognise what they can see and hear to be otherwise. Shakespeare is using the opportunity offered by the blending of different cultural discourses, high and low, to indicate the relativity of both. If the rude mechanicals are farcical to believe they can perform tragedy without reducing it to farce, so the socially distinguished characters are equally demonstrated as victims open to deceptions and misconstructions.

A Midsummer Night's Dream brings attention through its title to the play participating in an allowed moment of carnival. Midsummer was one of the five special festivals celebrated in London. It was a period when the carnival was sanctioned, the up-turning and parodying of social institutions allowed, so that official norms relinquished their power to a comic, unfixed view of the world. Midsummer festival allowed a licensed moment where a weaver and a queen commingling was conceivable, their social and cultural distinctions no longer observed. But the play, of course, did not have to be played at midsummer. It could be presented on the stage at any point. In considering the popular position of the stage within Elizabethan society, it has been noted that the theatre as a whole remained a licensed place where the norms of carnival might be enacted, regardless of whether it was a time of generally sanctioned festival or not. Discussing the place of the stage in Renaissance England, Steven Mullaney has drawn attention to the public theatre's situation in the Liberties outside London's city wall.[1] As the name implies, the

---

[1] Steven Mullaney, *The Place of the Stage: Licence, Play and Power in Renaissance England* (Chicago, University of Chicago Press, 1988).

Liberties were a place where the conditions and norms of behaviour practised within the City were not enforced. Mullaney notes how the Liberties were traditionally the site of institutions which the City needed, but which it could not tolerate within its walls (the leper houses of the Middle Ages are instanced). In the Renaissance, the theatres, too, became places where license was permitted.

What Mullaney also recognises though is a difference between, what might be called, medieval London, where the definitions of cultural space inscribed by ritual actions were widely recognisable and held in common, and the Renaissance city where a 'landscape of community' was becoming increasingly obscured. London's enhanced economic role in the country, the sudden rapid growth of its population, and its social organisation were changing, causing the city's symbolic role to be rendered opaque. Since the cultural sense of what Renaissance London represented was no longer generally recognised, Mullaney notes, there existed a need to provide vehicles which could help define the city's character. The theatres, Mullaney argues, became licensed spaces where such moral and cultural definitions could be established. This perspective parallels Peter Burke's belief in the separation between high and low cultural traditions taking place. What both reflect is that the time of the greatest outpouring of Renaissance drama was a cultural moment during which there no longer existed a clear consensus about what a theatre was and what it should accomplish. For Mullaney, this allowed the popular theatre, for a brief time, to achieve an ideological liberty. The theatre was constrained neither by a high cultural insistence that it adopt a unified voice which conformed to a social elite, nor by possessing a clearly defined role within the ritual life of the wider community. The theatre became a place which could dynamically generate ideas about the society it participated in, not only what that society was, but what it could and should be.

The theatre, thus, became a site where oppositional views could be enacted which transgressed the normally permitted social and cultural constraints of the community. Kings and peasants could occupy the same space and be seen mixing in ways not sanctioned in the real world. The norms by which powerful social institutions defined themselves could be contested. In *A Midsummer Night's Dream*, the duke Theseus agrees to hear the play Bottom and his fellows have organised for Theseus's marriage celebrations. Hippolyta his new queen is not happy about this prospect because she dislikes seeing those of lesser ability taking on more than they can properly perform, resulting in propriety being lost. Theseus, however, feels the lowness of the performers reflects well on his power:

> The kinder we, to give them thanks for nothing.
> Our sport shall be to take what they mistake;
> And what poor duty cannot do, noble respect
> Takes it in might, nor merit.
> Where I have come, great clerks have purposed
> To greet me with premeditated welcomes;
> Where I have seen them shiver and look pale,
> Make periods in the midst of sentences,
> Throttle their practis'd accent in their fears,
> And, in conclusion, dumbly have broke off,
> Not paying me a welcome. Trust me, sweet,
> Out of this silence yet I pick'd a welcome;
> And in the modesty of fearful duty
> I read as much as from the rattling tongue
> Of saucy and audacious eloquence.
> Love, therefore, and tongue-tied simplicity
> In least speak most, to my capacity.
>
> (V, i, 89–105)

Theseus has set up a series of imaginary preconceptions about the design and nature of the performance which are misplaced. The mechanicals are not playing out of duty or love of the Duke but in the hope of monetary reward. Their, equally misplaced, imaginary preconception is of a pension which means they will no longer have to work. More importantly, their performance demonstrates exactly the opposite of tongue-tied simplicity. They may make farce out of tragedy, but they are confident in their performance. Indeed, so confident that when Theseus makes a mocking observation about the figure playing the wall in the play, Bottom, thinking Theseus is taking everything seriously but is mistaking how the play is to be acted, corrects him: 'You shall see it will fall pat as I told you' (V, i, 184). Rather than being overwhelmed by Theseus's might, Bottom addresses the Duke familiarly. In allowing the play,

Theseus has unwittingly caused himself to participate in a world defined by the mechanicals' perceptions.

Theseus reveals that he creates an image of his powers based on criteria that the play travesties. He constructs categories about the lower classes with which they do not concur. In performing this play within a play, Shakespeare draws attention to the way that each class mistakenly imagines not only other social groups, but the terms on which classes define themselves. Rather than establishing a difference between high and low, *A Midsummer Night's Dream* reveals Theseus and the nobles to have a part in Bottom's play – contributing with their own asides as supposed spectators (but from our perspective as audience, as participants) to the debasement of the supposed tragedy of Pyramus and Thisbe. The categories which establish high and low, tragedy and farce are unfixed. The social structures which proposes that the better classes, with recourse to the institutions of high culture, perceive the world more accurately is revealed to be false. The higher classes and the rude mechanicals are both as open to enchantment, whether as victims of drugs or in their own imaginative misconstructions of themselves.

Bakhtin believed the world of carnival acted in a utopian fashion. In challenging the hierarchies created by official culture, he imagined festive misrule re-asserting the collective life of the popular community. He envisaged the wider community re-establishing its authority over the official culture of the elite through its demonstrating of the relativity of the norms of established authority. In many respects, a play such as *A Midsummer Night's Dream* appears to support aspects of the Bakhtinian analysis. But there are important differences, too. It is interesting to note that, as in *Doctor Faustus*, economic conditions are an important impetus to the lower orders to engage with the province of high culture. The clowns seek to imitate Faustus's arcane learning in magic and the mechanicals seek to put on a tragedy for Theseus because they imagine it will bring them economic betterment. In both cases the point is made forcefully by the modesty of their imagined rewards – the clowns will have enough to eat, the mechanicals sixpence a day.

While some plays reflect popular utopian desires of a more abundant life, either in looking forward or in recalling some memorable golden time, others present a much more sinister interaction between low and high culture. The English Renaissance theatre, if it sometimes liked to present itself as a place where social hierarchies and institutions might be unfixed, also explored more sinister implications of the way groups attempted to manipulate carnival conditions for their own particular ends. Shakespeare's *Henry IV* and *Henry V* offer good instances of a darker side to carnival. In *Henry IV*, Part I, the young Prince Hal makes a speech which bears superficial resemblances to Theseus's lines we considered above. Hal, too, sees the lowness of the popular a means through which he can represent his own superiority. But where Theseus misconstrued the designs of the lower classes, Prince Hal apparently has no such illusions:

> I know you all, and will awhile uphold
> The unyok'd humour of your idleness;
> Yet herein will I imitate the sun,
> Who doth permit the base contagious clouds
> To smother up his beauty from the world,
> That, when he please again to be himself,
> Being wanted, he may be more wond'red at
> By breaking through the foul and ugly mists
> Of vapours that did seem to strangle him.
> . . . .
> So, when this loose behaviour I throw off
> And pay the debt I never promised,
> By how much better than my word I am,
> By so much shall I falsify men's hopes;
> And, like bright metal on a sullen ground,
> My reformation, glitt'ring o'er my fault,
> Shall show more goodly and attract more eyes
> than that which hath no foil to set it off.
>
> (I, ii, 188–96; 201–8)

Hal's imagery reveals what he thinks of the masses, they are ugly and fouls mists. His revels with them are carefully organised to demonstrate himself ultimately a higher authority of a different kind. He is, he believes, as the sun and others of baser earthly mould. To convince others of his own self-imagining, he will play at being base for a time and then theatrically present himself in glory which 'shall show more goodly and attract more eyes'. Hal's revelry with Falstaff and his companions allows him to 'know them', a knowing which brings him to despise their idleness. What the play reveals is a manipulation of popular revelry by the elite for its own ends. As King Henry V, Hal rejects Falstaff utterly. He refuses even to allow he knows him, only acknowledging that he has dreamed of 'such a kind of man' (*Henry IV*, Part II, V, iv, 48–52). Henry's dalliance with the lower order, which raised their expectations of rewards, is over. Rather than creating a plural, unfixed perspective which questions the hierarchies of official culture, the prince's interactions with the lower orders and their festivity serve to enforce the rigours of official hierarchies. The popular only has a mistaken belief that its revelry influences the perception of social institutions. Allowing carnival is a means by which the elite confirm their own power and come to despise the lower classes. In a poignant moment of realisation, one of the starving citizens in Shakespeare's *Coriolanus* recognises that the nobles constitute their own abundance by keeping the lower order poor: 'the leanness that afflicts us, the object of our misery, is as an inventory to particularise their abundance; our sufferance is a gain to them' (I, i, 18–21).

How did a popular audience react to such revelations? The presentation of such a scene negated popular power in the wider community. Here were moments when the greater populace's roles within the culture was revealed as an instrument used by the social elites to manipulate and contain the popular. Shakespeare shows Prince Hal, and his later role as Henry V, to organise his actions according to norms which can be construed as Machiavellian in the desire to maintain authority. But Machiavelli intended his *Prince* for private perusal by the princely class the book was addressing, providing them with a manual of instruction, as it were. In Shakespeare's case, the audience was largely made-up of those whose Henry's machinations were directed against. In representing an English king manipulating the people for his own devices, the popular theatre may have not simply tacitly participated in a communally licensed playing, but acted as a determined voice of political opposition. More than offering linguistic and generic constructions which parodied the exclusive way high culture ordered the world, the Renaissance theatre also seems prepared to expose the basis by which a ruler controls social organisations. Prince Hal may be witnessed as a calculating power seeker, merely appearing popular in order to dupe both the lower classes and the elite so that his power might ultimately be manifested in a more absolute way. He is neither a ruler who genuinely participated in popular revelry, nor a prince, like Theseus, open to the same misconstructions of place which the popular shares. Rather than sharing in the life of a community, Hal helps undermine its organisation. He transgresses his place so that he can redefine it according to his own scheming ends.

In potentially casting Henry in this role, Shakespeare creates the conditions where the manipulation of appearances by ruling hierarchies are demystified for the audience, possibly encouraging popular opposition. Moving between popular and high cultural norms, and participating in a time of cultural transformation which was seeking a new coherence, the popular theatre was able to confront issues of social, political and wider cultural definition. It did not merely act to 'unfix' values from hierarchical institutions, but confronted the ways dominate institutions manipulated cultural values. The drama could even act to indicate new values.

If it is difficult to discover an organised programme of cultural redefinition in the drama, this is likely to be because of the volatile conditions of the time, a lack of consensus of what was now desired or even desirable. John Lyly, offering a justification of mixing comic and tragic genres, blames the stylistic confusion on the confusion within the times: 'If we present a mingle-mangle, our fault is to be excused, because the whole world is become an Hodge-podge'.[1] The result, though, is not necessarily one where the drama only reflected a lack of cultural definition by parodying those inherited from other institutions. The drama itself could re-define, but we should not expect its ideology to be singular and coherent.

III Will 'a tell us what this show meant?

In his notes on *Mother Courage*, Bertolt Brecht considers how he intended to ensure that his audience did not

[1] Cited in ibid., p. 19.

identify with Mother Courage.[1] She should not appear a heroine but a sad victim who has learned nothing. For Brecht, Courage exemplifies a historical contradiction, a figure whose source of 'livelihood', the war, is also the source of destruction of her family. What Brecht wished to stress was Courage's active participation in the war, that she was criminal in some sense. But Brecht noticed that audiences refused to see her that way. Rather they made her into a heroine, an inevitable victim of an occurrence perceived as natural. Brecht had intended the play to force the working classes to see that war was not inevitable and that resistance to it could abolish it. Instead his audiences were having their assumptions about the natural inevitability of war confirmed. Brecht also indicates that he recognises that this play he had written to organise the working classes against the bourgeois was actually performed before largely bourgeois audiences. It was a success with them becuse they interpreted it on their terms, believing it confirmed bourgeois indestructibility and power to survive. The audience interpreted the play according to a world-view perceived as natural, a view so powerfully established it enabled bourgeois audiences to celebrate a play designed to oppose accepting this world-view as actually participating in it and, indeed, reinforcing it.

Even with the opportunities open to the twentieth-century author writing within a specifically defined and widely acknowledged ideological framework it is apparently impossible to control the range of meanings inherent in a play. The drama's performance may not reflect intended meanings because of the manner of the playing, the constituency of the audience, or a combination of both. With Renaissance drama, where the opportunities for us to fathom the drama's intention are much more difficult to discern, we are left with a range of possibilities it is difficult to circumscribe.

A few years ago I gave a lecture to a group of sixth-formers on Shakespeare's *Measure for Measure*. I argued that the play-text leaves open possibilities for very different resolutions at the end. The lecture focused on the

[1] Bertolt Brecht, *Mother Courage and her Children*, John Willett (trans.), John Willett and Ralph Manheim (eds) (London, Eyre Methuen, 1980), pp. 143–7.

reaction of Isabella to the Duke's proposal of marriage. At the play's conclusion the Duke, who has concealed his identity to watch how his state is governed, reveals himself and apparently re-establishes his power. He dispenses his version of justice, apparently believing he has both re-established control in Vienna and acted rightly. His final speech is a summary of how his actions have brought concord where there was former strife. He concludes addressing Isabella:

> I have a motion much imports your good;
> Whereto if you'll a willing ear incline,
> What's mine is yours, and what yours is mine.
> So bring us to our palace, where we'll show
> What's yet behind that's meet you all should know.
>
> (V, i, 533–7)

J. W. Lever, the editor of the Arden edition, makes up a stage direction ('Exeunt Omnes') and a footnote to establish a closed ending to the play:

> A processional exit in pairs seem to be indicated by the dialogue; led by the Duke and Isabella; then Claudio and Juliet, Angelo and Mariana; Escalus and the Provost; Friar Peter and Barnardine; with Lucio under guard bringing up the rear.[1]

This editor is in no doubt that the play's conclusion agrees with the Duke's words, order and harmony have been restored, the conclusion is comic. But there is nothing to indicate that the Duke's words should have this authority in interpreting the play's actions. The Duke certainly tries to make things appear this way, but even the Duke recognises that Angelo's protestation of guilt and shame may be being offered as a contrived manoeuvre to save his life. When the Duke shows Claudio to be alive, whom Angelo believes he had executed in disgraceful circumstances, the Duke notes 'a quick'ning' in Angelo's eye which reveals Angelo now sees he is safe (V, i, 492). The Duke is prepared to accept Angelo's appearance of guilt because it reflects well on the Duke's appearance of power. He is not particularly concerned with whether

[1] William Shakespeare, *Measure for Measure*, J. W. Lever (ed.) (London, Methuen, 1965), p. 149.

Angelo is genuinely contrite. Similarly, Prospero at the conclusion of *The Tempest* wants his brother to behave contritely so that Prospero can behave magnanimously. In order to coerce his unrepentant brother to participate in the apparent reconciliations, Prospero details to both Sebastian and Antonio that he knows their plotted treachery against Alonso. Their feigned submission results from their fear of exposure, but what appears important is the semblance of harmony and merciful restitution which Prospero wants to be seen to have organised.

Angelo is clearly prepared to go along with the Duke's design as it is in his interest. But is Isabella? At the play's opening she is about to take her final vows as a nun. She has already chosen to be a bride of Christ, a higher authority than the Duke. What are her reactions to the Duke? She does not speak. The scene can be played in a variety of ways – Isabella can willingly comply, she can be startled, she can be affronted, she can be resigned and so forth. Any one of a variety of possibilities is open, none of which involves anything more than a final quick reaction but any one of which can substantially affect what we understand about the play. A sense that Isabella is coerced may have us feel the Duke only imagines he is acting as a true figure of Justice. Like Theseus in *A Midsummer Night's Dream* he projects a vision of his power which other aspects of the play reveal is misconceived. *Measure for Measure* is open to be concluded on a note of either festive comedy or near tragedy. What is clear, though, is that Isabella has to respond in some way – even if she barely responds at all. Performance does not allow a variety of endings to be rehearsed in the way literary criticism does. One possibility must be chosen, at least for each performance.

What I had wished to do in my lecture was to point out that critical endeavours which try to establish the superiority of one interpretation over the other are inevitably working with an incomplete sense of what the play can be. It was no good arguing that *Measure for Measure* 'really' should be played with one version of Isabella's reaction rather than another. What was interesting was that the play was left tantalisingly open but requiring completion. A completion which could be achieved only in performance since what was required was action not language. The 'meaning' of each performance of *Measure for Measure* was determined by actions which could only be written in a text as an elaborate stage direction, something Renaissance play-texts, as opposed to modern ones, never incorporate.

The students listened politely to my lecture, but when it came to questions they seemed unable to grasp what I was trying to say. They certainly saw that *Measure for Measure* could be conceived of as having multiple existences: as comedy, as tragedy, as neither. But what they wanted to know was what I *really* thought the play was about. In a sense they perceived my lecture rather like a performance of the play that just gave up somewhere toward the end because it could not bring itself to decide on how to conclude the play. Fine, it seemed they were saying to me, you have outlined how the play might be, now complete your critical performance as you would a dramatic performance – choose an ending. I could see their difficulty. They were going to be asked examination questions which would likely force them to choose and they wanted the 'expert' to choose for them. But it was like one of those book or film award programmes where the contenders' various excellent features are all reviewed while the audience waits to hear which one has won. All the contenders are said to be capable of being chosen. But then one is, and the audience's relation with all the books or films changes. Hierarchies are created, reputations made. No matter how the jury is disparaged, an ordered hierarchy it is difficult to counter has been founded.

Renaissance drama poses some powerful challenges to our critical practice. Establishing editorially prepared, authorised printed texts, a feature which on one hand helps to encourage the study of the drama, on the other helps to limit considerations of what the drama might be. What this exemplifies is a feature about Renaissance studies which our present age shares with the Tillyard generation of *The Elizabethan World Picture*, the apparently felt need to reduce the period to a few overriding considerations which provide categories and limits to the way cultural interpretation is conducted. As we have witnessed, one of the features which appears to give Renaissance drama a particular dynamism is its coinciding with a period when how drama was conceived was undergoing substantial change. Instead of trying to create elaborate chronological or cultural structures which map out dominant features on a field of change, we should perhaps be more concerned to concentrate on the varieties of possible interplay between cultural, social, political categories the drama explores. Rather than definitions about what plays are, or were at specific moments, we should perhaps be more concerned with the processes which promote indeterminacy. We should be more prepared to accept the implications of differences in the drama from other forms of writing and what this implies for the idea of the author, for the status of a text, for exploring relations between elite and popular generic resources. We need to confront the common critical technique of acknowledging differences between the drama and other literary representations, but then suspending, or tactfully ignoring, these differences when it comes to interpretive evaluation. What is clear is that the dynamics of the relation between popular and high culture, as well as the critical models we use for interpretation and analysis of drama, still require a great deal of energy expended on them.

7
Gendered Readings

In 'Elegy 19' John Donne takes his mistress to bed and explores her body:

> Licence my roving hands, and let them go
> Before, behind, between, above, below.
> O my America, my new found land,
> My kingdom, safeliest when with one man manned,
> My mine of precious stones, my empery,
> How blessed am I in thus discovering thee!
> To enter in these bonds, is to be free;
> Then where my hand is set, my seal shall be.[1]

Using the commonplace of the woman as the sovereign of her lover, Donne asks for a legal patent to explore her undiscovered territory. Just as the Virginia Company was given a royal mandate to colonise America, Donne wants entitlement to this woman. His explorations reveal that she is an unknown territory, a virgin. Her riches for Donne are increased in his knowledge that, as he mines her treasures, he will be free from the risk of veneral disease – she is 'safeliest when with one man manned'. In undertaking his ostensibly legalised explorations, Donne is gaining freedom to use his mistress undisturbed by the fear that she may be contaminated. There is no penalty to pay for his conquest and delight. Donne will conclude his successful diplomacy by formalising his negotiation, setting his seal (his penis) where his hands have been.

Donne's fantasy poses problems for the modern reader, raising questions about exploitation of the female arising from constructions of women by male authors. The jauntiness of Donne's wit in these lines is unlikely to be censored by readers because of assumptions about the woman's willing compliance. Such assumptions are possible because the woman is silent, she has no voice in the poem. Her place is created by the male author. Donne

---

[1] A. J. Smith (ed.), *John Donne: The Complete English Poems* (Harmondsworth, Penguin, 1971), p. 125. All citations from to Donne to Smith's edition.

implies his mistress possesses sovereignty to grant him the license to explore her, but he does not genuinely ask her permission or treat her as sovereign. Donne's hands are roving even as he requests a mandate, and, since roving means piracy, Donne is also bringing attention to his hands being outside the control of law. As is typical in Donne, a number of discourses converge. He effectively medically examines the woman, using the folkloric conventions that allow him to discover she is a virgin by finding her hymen intact. His examination offers him assurance that he will be free of the risk of disease in sexually possessing her. There are discourses of Renaissance colonisation, including the desires of English colonisers to find mineral riches in Virgina which would rival Spain's in South America. There is also the quasi-legal discourse associated with colonisa-tion and exploitation. Claiming he is licensed, Donne can take his mistress's wealth (her virginity) without fear of prosecution for theft or rape. Further, because Donne – as a rover – is outside the law, he has no real obligation to honour his bonds. Whether he possesses his mistress as a pirate takes a prize, or as the Virginia Company was granted a royal mandate to pursue its endeavours, Donne does not have any responsibility to his conquest. He remains free from obligations to her, even if his possession might cause her to imagine he now has duties towards her.

In this poetry of apparent praise and celebration of sexuality, Donne portrays masculine desires of conquest without responsibilities. His silent mistress apparently accepts the conditions. She is the open, undefended, virgin country awaiting possession by one man. Despite the poem being called 'Going to Bed' and beginning with the enjoinder of 'Come, Madam', Donne seems uninterested in his mistress as anything but a passive object around which he constructs his verse. This is not a private lyric in which readers feel they are voyeuristically intruding on an intimacy between two lovers. Instead, it is a public performance, addressed to a readership almost certainly envisaged to be male, showing Donne at play – sexually, but especially verbally – as the empowered male poet.

Inscribing the female from a male position such as Donne's can incite much critical hostility among current readers. Feminist criticism, the most powerful set of voices within current critical approaches to texts, have successfully promoted the importance of the female 'difference of view'. It has been feminists who have best articulated the existence of alternate ways of reading texts, and who have most effectively prompted readers to be aware of their own cultural preconceptions about gender when they consider representations of women and men in texts. Such has been the success of feminist criticism that those new to study may be almost unaware that it is only comparatively recently that most readers have realised that assumptions about gender roles presumed as 'natural' are, in fact, culturally learnt. The success of feminist critical perspectives has meant that most current readers 'naturally' see gender as creating crucial differences in the way women and men are represented in texts, and that such representations are culturally conditioned.

Feminists have drawn attention to the ways fictions of gender are created and how sexual identities are both enjoined and resisted by individuals and groups. Mary Jacobus, for example, has drawn attention to how a process of thinking about female difference reveals, not only the possibilities of rethinking the ways women are constructed in texts, but the ways in which writing itself may be re-presented. Jacobus sees a female literary tradition involving more than specifically 'female' domains which may be potentially confining:

> Rather, [a female literary tradition involves] a recognition that all attempts to inscribe female difference within writing are a matter of inscribing women within fictions of one kind or another . . . and hence, that what is at stake for both women writing and writing about women is the rewriting of these fictions – the work of revision which makes 'the difference of view' a question rather than an answer, and a question to be asked not simply of women, but of writing too.[1]

This difference of view has provoked some powerful readings of familiar Renaissance texts from unexpected perspectives. Coppelia Kahn, for instance, has considered

[1] Mary Jacobus, 'The difference of view', in Catherine Belsey and Jane Moore (eds) *The Feminist Reader: Essays in Gender and the Politics of Literary Criticism* (Basingstoke, Macmillan, 1989), pp. 61–2.

'The Absent Mother in King Lear'.[1] Examining the male social placing of women as figures who were supposed to remain silent in domestic environments divorced from the affairs of state, Kahn believes this to be a signal of a masculine need to repress the feelings of dependency and vulnerability the male also experiences. The male denies he possesses these emotional states because such experiences are associated with the feminine. Kahn locates in Lear a 'maternal subtext': 'the imprint of mothering on the male psyche, the psychological presence of the mother whether or not mothers are literally represented as characters'.[2] Kahn explores how this repressed mother surfaces in Lear's rage against his daughters, a rage she sees as directed against the absent mother. The rage brings about an upsetting of relations where parent–child, father–daughter and husband–wife relations are reversed and confounded. Lear's anger is seen leading to misogyny, which Kahn views as exemplifying patriarchal practices of attempting to deny the presence of the feminine in the male. Lear's confusions and rages lead to madness. It is only when he accepts the 'weeping woman' in himself that he is able to face Cordelia, who sees tears as a source of power not weakness.

As is clear from my summary of Kahn's analysis of Lear, techniques used in psychoanalysis are being employed to treat Lear as a case study of a particular psychological condition. Psychoanalysis has been perceived in many circles as essential to feminism, in that it challenges easy assumptions about sexual identity and, most importantly, reveals that there are resistances to identities which are culturally enjoined. Jacqueline Rose has argued that: 'Viewed in this way, psychoanalysis . . . becomes one of the few places in our culture where it is recognised as more than a fact of individual pathology that most women do not painlessly slip into their roles as women'.[3] As Kahn shows with King Lear, this is true of men and male roles, too. Implications of gender are, therefore, seen as providing important insights into how individuals contend with the

[1] Coppelia Kahn, 'The Absent Mother in *King Lear*', in *Rewriting the Renaissance*, op. cit., pp. 33–49 (see Chapter 2, note 9).
[2] Ibid., p. 35.
[3] Jacqueline Rose, *Sexuality in the Field of Vision* (London, Verso, 1986), p. 91.

social forces which try to define them in ways incompatible with their unconscious.

Lacan called the unconscious, 'the other scene', and it is, perhaps, not surprising that techniques drawn from psychoanalysis have powerfully informed feminist attempts to find 'the difference of view'.[1] The unconscious is the place where resistances to dominant cultural and social orders can be located. In the Renaissance, these orders are unquestionably equated with patriarchy, the Law of the Father. It is appropriate, therefore, that techniques which examine the unconscious are able to find alternatives to a masculine dominance not only of social institutions, but of language. One of the difficulties feminist criticism recognises is that Renaissance language, even when employed by women writers, is dominated by masculine preconceptions.

In the Renaissance, masculine dominance of language was reinforced by the emphasis put on the Word of God, a decidedly male creator whose language was discovered in Scripture. A telling anecdote illustrates this. In Germany, the wife of a printer rebelled against the sentence of subjection to her husband imposed by Genesis 3:16 ('thy [the woman's] desire shall be to thy husband, and he shall rule over thee'). The printer's wife substituted two letters in the German text – he shall be thy *Herr* (master) became he shall be thy *Narr* (fool). For this blasphemy the wife was put to death.[2] The anonymous T. E., author of *The Lawes Resolutions of Women's Rights* (1632), considering how man and woman are made one person in marriage, suggests that the arrangement is to be understood on the analogy of how a small brook (the woman) becomes incorporated into a major river: 'the poor rivulet loseth her name . . . it beareth not sway; it possesseth nothing. . . . I may . . . say to a married woman her new self is her superior, her companion, her master'.[3] T. E. acknowledges how both the English legal framework and interpretations of Scripture made common cause in reducing the position

[1] For an introduction to Lacan see Malcolm Bowie, 'Jacques Lacan', in John Sturrock (ed.), *Sturcturalism and Since: from Levi-Strauss to Derrida* (Oxford, Basil Blackwell, 1979), pp. 116–53.

[2] Cited in James Grantham Turner, *One Flesh: Paradisal Marriage and Sexual Relations in the Age of Milton* (Oxford, Clarendon Press, 1987), p. 98.

[3] Cited in Graham *et al.* (eds) Her Own Life, op. cit., p. 7 (see Chapter 3, note 14).

of woman: 'The common law here shaketh hand with divinity.' Women are perceived as property, their desires wholly subject to men.

When Renaissance women wrote, therefore, they were aware that they were undertaking an activity which was perceived as a masculine domain. Few women, of course, had access to education. Even those who did, frequently found themselves denied the instruction which would allow them to present themselves as intellectually equal with men. Rhetoric and its training in the public arts of expression was commonly denied women, whose proper sphere was considered the private and domestic, not the public world of debate. Women's education was in areas largely designed to complement male activity, not emulate the masculine province. Music, needlework, some reading and writing were felt useful skills, but the pattern of instruction and the texts examined were designed to promote traditional feminine attributes: obedience, loyalty and maintenance of female honour, notably chastity. The ideal Renaissance woman was usually portrayed as the silent woman within the household. To speak out, even in print, was to suggest a certain wantonness and lack of chastity. As Constance Jordan has suggested, to even talk of 'famous women' was almost a contradiction in terms.[1] Women in a public dimension were almost always either infamous or fantastic – as a sex, they were not supposed to gain public attention.

An excellent example of the difficulties faced by the woman writer is presented by Margaret Cavendish, Duchess of Newcastle writing in the mid-seventeenth century. As her social title indicates, Cavendish's experience was hardly typical of Renaissance women. Cavendish took the significant step of publishing an account of her life, *A True Relation of my Birth, Breeding and Life*, which was appended to a collection of her stories published in 1656. Cavendish acknowledges that in writing she is intruding on to masculine territory and will be attacked by male readers: 'because they think thereby women encroach too much upon their prerogatives; for they hold books as their

---

[1] Constance Jordan, *Renaissance Feminism: Literary Texts and Political Models* (Ithaca, Cornell University Press, 1990), p. 35.

crown, and the sword as their sceptre, by which they rule and govern'.[1] It is interesting that she conjoins the pen and the sword rather than opposing them. Both become instruments which suggest repression, potentially violent, of the female.

Margaret Cavendish's account of her life gives a vivid illustration of how an intelligent woman was forced to live according to male conceptions, which interpreted a readiness to participate in public activities as 'forwardness' in women. She recounts how she persuaded her mother to let her become a maid of honour to the Queen (Henrietta Maria) and go to live at Court:

I had heard the world was apt to lay aspersion even on the innocent, for which I durst neither look up with my eyes, nor speak, nor be any way sociable: insomuch as I was thought a natural fool. Indeed I had not much wit, yet I was not an idiot; my wit was according to my years. And though I might have learnt more wit and advanced my understanding by living in a court, yet being dull, fearful and bashful, I neither heeded what was said or practised, but just what belonged to my loyal duty and my own honest reputation. And indeed I was so afraid to dishonour my friends and family by my indiscreet actions, that I rather chose to be accounted a fool, than to be thought rude or wanton.

(p. 90)

Throughout her *True Relation* Margaret Cavendish reveals the problems for women whose identity is defined through men. She argues that the principal reason she writes is to 'tell the truth' of herself, a truth which she feels is important to record because otherwise her identity, conferred through her male parent and her husband, might be lost:

Lest after ages should mistake, in not knowing I was daughter to one Master Lucas of St John's near Colchester in Essex, second wife to the Lord Marquis of Newcastle; for my lord having had two wives, I might easily have been mistaken, especially if I should die and my lord marry again.

(p. 99)

---

[1] Margaret Cavendish, in Graham *et al.* (eds) *Her Own Life*, op. cit., p. 88. All citations to Cavendish from this edition.

In contrast to her apparent acceptance of her husband remarrying if she should die, she praises her mother's constancy in not marrying again after her father's death: 'She made her house her cloister, enclosing herself, as it were, therein' (p. 91). Her mother was affectionate: 'breeding her children with a most industrious care and love . . . there was not any one crooked or any ways deformed' (p. 92). The ideal woman emerges as a silent domestic figure, who is a good breeder and is defined by her duties to her male 'governor'.

The social conditions of women during the early modern period has prompted some current writers to ask whether women had a Renaissance at all. Those aspects of the early modern world which are hailed as cultural achievements appear almost wholly the preserve of males. If Hamlet feigns madness and discovers something of subjectivity, Ophelia is driven mad through the males in her life denying her any role except derangement – she becomes the daughter of a dead father, the rejected lover of the prince. But a wholly negative assessment of the impact of the Renaissance on women is far too severe. As Margaret Cavendish's writings demonstrate, women were able to mount resistances. Although acknowledging that she is invading male territory by writing at all, Cavendish pleads that hers is a revelation of truth:

> But I verily believe some censuring readers will scornfully say, why hath this lady writ her own life? Since none cares to know whose daughter she was, or whose wife she is, or how she was bred, or what fortunes she had . . . I answer that it is true, that 'tis no purpose to the readers but it is to the authoress, because I write it for my own sake, not theirs. Neither did I intend this piece for to delight, but to divulge; not to please the fancy, but to tell the truth.
>
> (pp. 98–9)

Denying her account in *A True Relation* the status of high literature (which according to Sidney's *Defence of Poetry* should teach *and* delight), Cavendish is also asserting her presence, and that of women as a gender. By breaking silence, she is demonstrating that women can be a part of written culture – this fact cannot be denied because of her voice. Her life is offered as a piece of truth. To criticise its limitations, both in its telling and in its content, is to suggest she should be untruthful. This insistence on her accurate rendering of her life asserts her life's authentic place within written culture, though acknowledging it does not easily fit in with the male organisation of literary culture.

Interestingly, in adopting this approach Cavendish is also aligning herself with the developing forms of spiritual autobiography (of which Richard Baxter's *Autobiography* and John Bunyan's *Grace Abounding* are the best known examples). In this sub-genre, the assertion of experiential truth as a defence for the writing of the life is a familiar feature. Claims to be authentically witnessing the divine justifies the supposed unpolished style which is used to record often humble experiences, with the implication that polished stylistic eloquence is questionable in present-ing truth. Earlier, in discussing the problems of Milton's *Samson Agonistes* as a text divorced from a potentially sym-pathetic readership because of its style (Chapter 1), we saw how high literary culture was frequently suspect to men and women disenfranchised from it because of birth, edu-cation or religious conviction. During the mid-seventeenth century, largely as a result of the Civil War, these new voices from below gained greater access to written culture. Women could use techniques also being employed by men to criticise cultural practices.

A voice such as Margaret Cavendish's is not forced to confront high cultural norms on the grounds that they are exclusively masculine, a position which might serve only to emphasise female difference in a manner which would make it seem marginal. Rather, by aligning herself with a technique 'godly', mostly Puritan, men were also adopting, Cavendish is able to voice criticism of a type of written culture which some men were also opposing. One of the features of the Reformation was the emphasis put on achieving individual salvation. The example of the godly individual became an important repository of moral *exempla*. Within Protestanism, accounts of people's dis-covery of the divine in themselves replaced saints lives as a vehicle for encouraging religious devotion. As Elaine Beilin notes, this allowed women to represent virtues associated with their sex, such as chastity and humility, not merely

as the features of the weak female, but as the qualities of
the good Christian.[1]

Importantly, Cavendish's voice of opposition is not only
located in casting suspicions on an elite masculine written
culture through confronting its norms. She also subtly
resists the male and established culture's objection that
her female truth is not worth recording, is not worthily a
part of written culture, by locating herself within a powerful classical tradition. Despite her qualifications of her
endeavours, she finally asserts her cultural presence not
as an oddity but as within the mainstream of a Renaissance
tradition of eloquence. In a plea that her readers will
not think her 'vain' in writing her life and, therefore,
exemplifying an immodest, infamous woman, Cavendish
recalls that many other writers have written their lives: 'as
Caesar, Ovid and many more, both men and women, and
I know no reason I may not do it as well as they' (p. 98).
Answering her 'censuring readers' (either men or women
reacting according to patriarchal norms), Margaret Cavendish is able to expose the contradictions of patriarchal
criticism through a shrewd logic. Powerful, admired male
writers have written similarly (Caesar exemplifying the
active male, Ovid the stylistically eloquent one). It cannot
be improper to write one's life. Margaret Cavendish is
able to make an equation between herself and classically
admired writers, while proposing that she is aware of
the difference of scope between their environment and
her private female one. Further, as we see, her account
contains the premise, and implicit criticism, that such male
lives (Caesar's and Ovid's included) are designed to please
the fancy and delight, not primarily to divulge the truth. If
male lives are more interesting in event and in the telling,
women's lives may be rendered more accurately. Women's
lives are not the 'pleasing fictions' through which male
lives are consummated to be read as literature. The necessary adoption of masculine cultural and linguistic norms
by Renaissance women writers should not obscure that
they could employ these norms critically. Through skilful
deployment of male dominated language, women could

---

[1] Elaine V. Beilin, *Redeeming Eve: Women Writers of the English Renaissance* (Princeton,
Princeton University Press, 1987) p. xv.

subtly reveal its limitations and contradictions. Women were not forced to celebrate uncritically male dominated cultural practices.

Examples such as Margaret Cavendish show that we do not need only to look to 'the other scene' of the unconscious to find resistances to masculine domination of the feminine. Yet, we must also be careful in presenting the limited number of examples of women writers who challenged male assumptions in such a way that they distort the general cultural conditions women contended with. Selected examples of powerful female voices can achieve a representative status which suggests a much more organised resistance than is likely to have been the case. The small number of women who were writing may be disproportionately employed by modern readers in determining women's position in Renaissance culture. If it is common to find Renaissance male writers exaggerating female unruliness in the culture to validate their fears of feminine disorder and justify repressive moves against women, we should also be wary of suggesting those few women who were able to voice resistance had a widespread impact on attitudes. Much fundamental work on the position of women in early modern society is still being undertaken. We rightly celebrate those female voices who broke partiarchally imposed silences, but we should not ignore the often grim conditions of the vast majority who were forced to endure in silence. The most recent editors of Margaret Cavendish's *A True Relation* record how this account of her life was removed from the second edition of the collection to which it had been appended in 1656.[1] Although her own account of herself was brief, as the editors note, it was silenced after she had written a full-length biography of her husband.

Clearly, educated noblewomen such as Margaret Cavendish and more humble women, such as the printer's wife in the anecdote from Germany, were not prepared to accept their roles as defined by a male patriarchy, even when these roles were apparently supported by Scripture. Yet, as both examples illustrate, resistances were hard to organise and could be brutally silenced (the printer's wife executed) as

[1] *Her Own Life*, op. cit., p. 89.

well as more quietly censored (Cavendish's life disappears from print). One of the questions we are faced with is how should we critically explore representations of women in the Renaissance? Do we look for those writers who, in some respect, anticipated the present in allowing women some equality of presence? Alternatively, should we seek out texts which represent the widespread repressions of women because they indicate more accurately the conditions of the time? Further, and perhaps more importantly, how do we read representations of gender in Renaissance texts? Do we seek, as critics, somehow to colonise these texts with our meanings, reading through them so that they provide evidence of controversies or desires which are ours, rather than those of the past? Or do we seek to sit magisterial in judgement on the Renaissance, condemning the supposed errors in its beliefs about gender and its representations of gender problems?

As we have witnessed throughout this book, the implications of these questions are ones which we apply to all areas of critical concern, not simply questions of gender. But it is gender debates, and particularly the representation of women, which have excited extensive comment. Gillian Beer has noted how it is easy from a current perspective to offer 'inquisitorial reading of past literature', looking for correctness and error according to current perspectives on gender relations.[1] As she argues, the problem is that we become cast as inquisitors somehow outside history: 'like those late nineteenth-century doctors who described their patients and yet exempted themselves from the processes of disease and decay they describe' (p. 69). Rather, Beer argues, we should not be so concerned to read through texts but respect their difference, 'to revive those shifty significations which do not pay court to our concerns but are full of the meaning of that past present' (p. 68). Beer is concerned to understand how gender formations develop within a culture, how representations become representative – claiming authority in what they claim to present as authentic. Her concern is to demonstrate how change takes place, to reveal assumptions which seem natural and permanent as temporary and learnt.

[1] Gillian Beer, 'Representing women: re-presenting the past', in *The Feminist Reader*, op. cit., pp. 63–80.

The difference of the past is important: 'it will challenge
. . . the notion of a stable archetypal order' (p. 65).
Beer's emphasis on historical difference is an important objection, iterated by other historicist critics of
psychoanalytic models of feminist analysis of Renaissance
texts. One difficulty with Kahn's analysis of *King Lear*
(though not, I should emphasise, an overriding objection)
is that it is in part forced to approach the characters as
real people, perceived living largely under transhistorical
psychological conditions. Kahn's critical orientation largely
counters a historicist view which witnesses the play's
characters as fictional respresentations produced from
within a specific historical culture.[1] These representations,
both of men and women, are usually produced by male
authors, which, in itself, makes it difficult to analyse
female characters as though they were somehow 'really
women'. Further, historicist critics point out that such
characters were unlikely to have been fashioned to
explore conditions of interior characterisation. They may
not actually have been conceived with any presumption of
achieving psychological accuracy in their representation.
Representations of sexuality may have been intended
to express social conditions rather than an internal
psychology.

Women in Renaissance writing are frequently portrayed
as inferior men. They became sites where disruptive social
fears were located. Posthumous's assertion in *Cymbeline*
that: 'For there's no motion/That tends to vice in man
but I affirm/It is the woman's part' (III, i, 20–1) is not
merely a revelation of misogyny. It is a reflection on qualities
which were part of a gendered hierarchy of characteristics
in which both sexes shared. The female part was believed to
represent uncontrolled emotion, disruptive sexuality and
intellectual deficiency; the male denoted order, power,
restraint. Chastising a painter who depicted St Teresa
having her heart pierced by an angel with a fiery spear,
Richard Crashaw claims the painter has belittled her:
'One would suspect thou meant'st to paint/Some weak,
inferiour, woman saint'.[2] Instead, Crashaw advocates

---

[1] See esp. Jardine, *Still Harping on Daughters*, op. cit., pp. 1–8.
[2] L. C. Martin, editor, *The Poems English Latin and Greek of Richard Crashaw*, 2nd ed
(Oxford, Clarendon Press, 1957), p. 325

that Teresa's masculine immortal qualities be recognised. Though acknowledging she is female, Crashaw does not see St Teresa as feminine in emotion and attacks the painter who has inappropriately presented her as being too completely a woman: 'this speakes pure mortall frame;/And mockes with female FROST loue's manly flame'. If Renaissance male writers rarely allow women to exhibit superior 'masculine' qualities, it was believed possible that women could attain such qualities.

Looking at Renaissance drama, it is noticeable that women who give in to sexual urges outside of marriage are usually portrayed as unruly in a wider social sense. In *Arden of Faversham*, Alice's desire for Mosby leads to her husband's murder (in dramatic representations, a common consequence of women giving up marital chastity). In suspecting her liaison with another man, what particularly offends her husband is Alice's lack of social decorum in carrying on with a man who is socially inferior to the Ardens. At the play's conclusion, the sentencing of Alice, Mosby and their accomplices demonstrate the authorities reasserting the social order generally, not simply punishing a domestic disruption.

Similarly, the Duchess's brothers in Webster's *The Duchess of Malfi* feel justified in terrorising the Duchess about re-marriage because they fear such an act will bring disgrace upon their family. They may be psychologically unhinged and incestuously jealous at the prospect of her re-marrying but, at the time of the play's composition in the early seventeenth century, society would have recognised their anxieties about disruption to family honour and the inheritance of property. The Duchess's secret marriage to her socially inferior steward acts to support a widely held view that women are not to be trusted because they are victims of their emotions. Swayed by emotional appetites which they were generically believed to be more prone to than men, women were imagined unable to maintain the reasonable boundaries felt necessary for the maintenance of social order. They needed the proper government of men, if they were to keep their right place in a civilised society.

In Thomas Heywood's *A Woman Killed with Kindness*, Anne Fairfax readily succumbs to her husband's friend,

Wendoll. There is no attempt to explain her easy seduction, nothing in the play which indicates that she is likely to commit adultery. The implication appears to be that as a woman, Anne is generically likely to be enticed through emotional appeals. It appears only to be expected that she succumbs easily to Wendoll's persuasion. A commonplace in Renaissance attacks on women was that Eve readily succumbed to Satan's temptations, resulting in all human misery. The cultural expectation was that women were likely to be easily corrupted. Anne Fairfax's 'fall' causes her husband's household to be disrupted. The play concentrates on the guilt resting with the corrupted woman, not the corrupter Wendoll. If women were believed to be easily tempted, they were also readily imagined as temptresses. 'Fie upon women! this shall be my song' announces Mosby after being sentenced to die for his part in the murder of Arden.[1] The commonplace representation was that, if women's emotional instability caused transgression of social boundaries, it was the provocative female rather than the provoked male who was fundamentally responsible for the disruptive consequences.

What is apparent is that, besides being people, women in the Renaissance were also commonly represented as 'mobile property'. They needed to be governed and kept in place if society is to be maintained in a civil fashion. While the deceitful quality of women is constantly articulated, notably a fear in their power to betray their governors, it is also clear that a male inability to rule properly is a weakness which is being severely criticised throughout the period. The literature discloses not simply female disruptions, but male disorders, a masculine inability for rational self-control even among the governing aristocracy. Middleton's play *Women Beware Women*, for example, concludes with the female characters engaging in a sequence of destruction, the results of various emotional entanglements. Bianca, who has been allured out of her marriage by the Duke of Florence, ends up poisoning herself after having mistakenly poisoned the Duke. In her death, she represents herself as symbolic of feminine sexual destructiveness: 'Learn by me/To know your foes.

[1] Keith Sturgess (ed.), *Three Elizabethan Domestic Tragedies* (Harmondsworth, Penguin, 1969), p. 147.

In this belief I die:/Like our own sex, we have no enemy'
(V, ii, 211–13).[1] This proposal that women are enemies
to all, including themselves, concludes a series of female
instigated destructive acts which have reduced Florentine
society to confusion. But it is the Cardinal in the play,
as the surviving male, who has the last words. He does
not continue the theme of the evils of unruly women,
rather drawing attention to them as the result of male
defectiveness, the inability to govern properly. If lust and
sin exhibit themselves in women, the Cardinal's use of
'king' and 'his' propose that Sin within Middleton's drama is
finally conceived as possessing a male identity. The Duke,
having given way to sexuality, is actually responsible for
the confusion which has swept through his court and
brought destruction to his people:

> Sin, what thou art, these ruins show too piteously!
> Two kings on one throne cannot sit together
> But one must needs down, for his title's wrong:
> So where lust reigns, that prince cannot reign long.
>
> (V, ii, 220–4)

The epilogue of *Arden of Faversham* has Arden's friend,
Franklin, reminding the audience that Arden had been
guilty of appropriating land from its rightful owners in
shady property deals. Arden was a rising bourgeois, who
looked to increase his estate through dealing in former
Church lands. The implication is that his own socially
disruptive practices are mirrored in his inability to have
his own property, his wife, observe social decorums.

Condemnations of a male lack of government, exemplified by an inability to control the female, can be found
iterated throughout early modern English society. A mayor
of York whose wife was a Roman Catholic recusant was
summoned before the High Commission and told 'that
he is unmete to governe a cittie that can not governe
his own household'.[2] This characterising of male order
and female disorder helps explain the attempts to represent Queen Elizabeth as a symbolic representation of
virtue, not as a sexual being open to female disruptiveness.

---

[1] Roma Gill, 'Women beware women', in Roma Gill (ed.) *Elizabethan and Jacobean Tragedies*
(Tonbridge, Ernest Benn, 1984).
[2] Cited in Conrad Russell, *The Causes of the English Civil War* (Oxford, Clarendon Press,
1990), p. 67.

Elizabeth 'stood in for the male', she made no attempt
to challenge received partriarchal structures. Yet, as we
witnessed with Spenser's *Faerie Queene* in a previous chapter, writers experienced uncomfortable accommodations
with Elizabeth's sex. She could be tolerated only as an
exception:

> But vertuous women wisely understand,
> That they were borne to base humilitie
> Unless the heavens lift them to lawfull soveraintie
> *(Faerie Queene* V. V. 25)

Only as a divinely appointed monarch could Elizabeth's
role as sovereign be approved within the male ordered
structures of government. One strategy of 'explaining'
Elizabeth, was to suggest that she exemplified how God
'worked in strange ways'. The Divine's sense of wonder
and mystery extended even to allowing a woman to
be a proper monarch. It is not clear how far such
arguments were believed, even if they were publicly
accepted. It is interesting to note how James I promoted
the idea of fatherly monarchs in response to Elizabeth,
emphasising his supposed proper patriarchal rule of the
country founded on the model of the male governor of
his family. But Stuart claims to masculine rule, however,
were attacked by Charles I's opponents, who condemned
him for being too much influenced by his Roman Catholic
wife, Henrietta Maria. Milton is uncompromising in his
view of Charles's femininity:

> How great mischief and dishonour hath befall'n to Nations
> under the Government of effeminate and Uxorious Magis-
> trates, who being themselves govern'd and overswaid at
> home under a Feminine usurpation cannot be farr short
> of spirit and authority without dores, to govern a whole
> Nation.[1]

Elizabethan presentations of the Queen as 'masculine',
indicates that gender was perceived as a category for
representing certain qualities, not simply sexual identity.
In dealing with Renaissance drama, therefore, we should
not automatically assume characters are realistic men and
women, instead of representations of certain qualities,

---

[1] Cited in *One Flesh*, op. cit., p. 223.

virtues and vices associated with the male or the female. This has implications for the expectations of literary experience created in texts. Marlowe's *The Tragedy of Dido, Queen of Carthage*, for example, re-orients the masculine heroic ethos of Virgil's epic *The Aeneid* in which the Dido story originates. Marlowe's title's recognition of the drama centring on the female brings attention to the feminine dilemma of uncontrolled emotion (shared by both male and female characters), which is the centre of the play's concern. Within Virgil's *Aeneid*, the Dido story is an episode, revealing the hero Aeneas not yet matured but still undergoing heroic education in his ideal role as the founder of Roman destiny. The leaving of Dido is portrayed as a sadly necessary but ultimately positive action, demonstrating that Aeneas is accepting the will of divine destiny, achieving stature through self-sacrifice. In Marlowe's play the concentration is on the emotional instability of both Dido and Aeneas, a drama with a 'feminine' (emotionally uncontrolled) perspective.

In the *Aeneid*, the presentation of Dido and Aeneas maintains an epic imperial dimension in which to place their episode. The grand design of fate in the *Aeneid* is revealed by Jove who, as enthroned majesty, directs destiny with elevated epic grandeur. Marlowe's *Dido* transforms this Virgilian perspective, undermining the Virgilian cosmic framework. The play opens with Jupiter (Jove) and Ganymede (a beautiful boy who, in mythology, Jupiter abducted and made his catamite). Any expectation of Jupiter fulfilling his role of Virgilian guardian of high destiny is quickly deflated by the frivolous erotic banter between the god and his minion. At points, Jupiter attempts to use the rhetoric of epic and put on his role as *magister*, but this merely emphasises how the heroic ethos has collapsed under the erotic stress of Ganymede. The god appears as an emotional captive and irresponsibly foolish, placing the boy on his knee and inviting him to 'Control proud Fate and cut the thread of Time' (I, i, 29). Ganymede, with the heavens and earth to choose from, only selects a jewel for his ear and a brooch for his hat.

Beginning *Dido, Queen of Carthage* in this way, Marlowe reinforces the emphasis of the title on feminine preoccupations. Changes in a text's centre of interest from a prior text it is imitating are signalled by changes in form. Love 'Began to smile and tooke one foote away', so Marlowe interprets Ovid from the *Amores* to indicate the shift in substance caused by a change from epic hexameter to English blank verse.[1] Rhyme, we should recall, is still gendered as masculine and feminine in literary terminology. Writers could exploit literary expectations derived from genre to create expectations for the deployment of gender in texts. The Renaissance, for instance, continued the classical tradition of reducing masculine epic to feminine epyllia (little epics or 'scraps of poetry'). The epyllia's thematic concentrations on masculine degeneracy wrought by the emotional entanglements of feminine sensuality (Marlowe's *Hero and Leander* and Shakespeare's *Venus and Adonis* are the best known examples) is stylistically mirrored by the reduction of epic form. But if the style and substance of the epyllion was seen as reduction from a masculine fullness achieved in epic, there was also a recognition that epic itself could be seen composed of the epyllia's 'scraps of poetry'. The province of feminine poetry might lack the completion and order imagined in masculine forms, but the feminine helped ultimately compose the masculine. As such the feminine held the potential to compromise the masculine. The high and noble male style might be undermined by intruding feminine preoccupations.

Marlowe's *Dido, Queen of Carthage*, by demonstrating the highest god undermined by sexuality, slipping into apparent degeneracy through uncontrolled emotion, asserts a challenge to beliefs about the supposed force of male order which is celebrated as properly shaping and dominating human experience. Masculine control is seen to give way easily to feminine instability, even with the most pre-eminent examples of classical masculinity and male virtues. What is significant is that Marlowe depicts this female emotional instability as not being necessarily caused by women but, in the case of Jupiter, by a boy. Similarly, in *Edward II*, Marlowe shows that the king's desire for private emotional solace with his male friend/lover Gaveston undermines his ability to govern the

---

[1] C. F. Tucker Brooke (ed.), *The Works of Christopher Marlowe* (Oxford, Clarendon Press, 1910), p. 559.

kingdom. Edward's refusal of masculine responsibility and the male public sphere in favour of private feminine sensual indulgence brings the whole kingdom into civil conflict. As witnessed with the Crashaw example above, the category of the masculine could be open to women. With Marlowe, we have instances of the feminine being open to men. In recognising this latter possibility, Renaissance writing commonly sounds a note of fear.

Even when apparently praising the power of the female, male anxiety about the disruptive quality of feminine sexuality is readily perceived. Sidney's Astrophil shows that Stella's supposed positive, ennobling, influence over him also unmans him so that he forgets his male province of martial virtue. In sonnet 53 of *Astrophil* and *Stella*, Astrophil details how at a jousting tournament he was winning the day in 'Martiall sports', the result of 'Youth, luck, and praise'. But Astrophil is distracted seeing Stella in a window:

> My heart then quaked, then dazzled were mine eyes,
> One hand forgot to rule, th'other to fight;
> Nor trumpet's sound I heard, nor friendly cries;
> My foe came on, and beat the air for me,
> Till that her blush taught me my shame to see.

Donne held that Eve was created from a male rib in order to demonstrate how women weaken men.[1] Milton's *Samson Agonistes* has the male hero castigating feminine sexuality which distracts men from divine purposes and leads to their being rendered physically incapacitated. Spenser's *Faerie Queene* is constantly showing how false women corrupt men through sensually undermining them. Even among writers who apparently celebrate women for their beauty and grace, there exists a fear that female sexuality will cause the male to sink into effeminacy.

Importantly, though, there are instances in Renaissance writing where female virtues become actively sought, and indeed appropriated by masculine writers. This is the least examined feature of current discussions of Renaissance gender. As we have seen, it is assumed that Renaissance female writers were forced to accept, or at least acknowledge, dominate masculine norms when projecting

[1] See *One Sex*, op. cit., pp. 194–5; 225–6.

feminine identity. In contrast, male writers are usually seen to displace the importance of the female by reducing feminine representations to a few negative stereotypes. As a result, it can sometimes seem that a feminist 'diference of view' may be located only by reading through male authored texts from a late twentieth-century perspective, looking for significant suppressions, evasions, and contradictions in texts. There do, however, appear contemporary exceptions to the usual pattern of female representations among male authors.

Milton's *Paradise Lost* is an important instance of male appropriation of virtues seen as distinctly feminine. Initially, Milton's depiction of Eve in the early books of the poem seems to confer on her a status recognisable within familiar male limits set for female representation during the period. In Book IV, for instance, Milton details the circumstances of Eve's creation. She is presented as the innocent, without a true ability to distinguish between truth and falsehood. Adam 'by quick instinctive motion' jumped up at his creation 'as thitherward endeavouring' (VIII, 259–60), revealing his natural inclination towards heaven. Eve, in contrast, is led by the murmur of water to look at herself in a pool and narcissistically becomes enchanted with her own image. She needs the intervention of God the Father to direct her to Adam. She has to learn to appreciate his superiority, it is not something she appears capable of intuitively appreciating. A 'proper' recognition of the poem's hierarchy of creation is not spontaneously experienced by Eve. Only when Adam asserts his claim to her and exercises his strength of control over her does she recognise true order: 'and from that time see/How beauty is excelled by manly grace/And wisdom, which alone is truly fair' (IV, 489–91).

The result appears a male fantasy. Eve's beauty and sensuality is enhanced by her compliance with Adam, a state of affairs which, as the voyeur Satan's hateful torment in watching it confirms, is Milton's idea of a divine harmony between man and woman:

> our general mother, and with eyes
> Of conjugal attraction unreproved,
> And meek surrender, half embracing leaned
> On our first father; half her swelling breast

Naked met his under the flowing gold
Of her loose tresses hid; he in delight
Both of her beauty and submissive charms,
Smiled with superior love,

(IV, 492–9)

Satan's discovery of Eve separated from Adam allows him
to entice her to the Fall. Milton presents the independent
Eve as undefended. She is imagined, recalling Donne's
discovery of his mistress, as a new found land, a vulnerable
natural entity. Milton's iconography reveals Eve incorrectly
absent from Adam. By binding up the drooping flowers her
own actions show the need of interdependency and mutual
support she has foregone in leaving Adam. Yet, just as
Satan is delighted in the separate Eve, Milton reveals
a enticement with the unsupported female, sensual and
alluring because vulnerable:

Eve separate he spies,
Veiled in a cloud of fragrance, where she stood,
Half spied, so thick the roses bushing round
About her glowed, oft stooping to support
Each flower of slender stalk, whose head, though gay
Carnation, purple, azure, or specked with gold,
Hung drooping unsustained; them she upstays
Gently with myrtle band, mindless the while,
Herself, though fairest unsupported flower,
From her best prop so far, and storm so nigh.

(IX, 424–33)

What Milton then does in *Paradise Lost* is to redeploy Eve's
vulnerability and dependency after the Fall, so that these
qualities become exemplary of the condition of humanity.
He then employs the female to indicate the means by
which the degeneracy which has resulted from the Fall
may be reversed. At the beginning of Book IX of *Paradise
Lost*, Milton claims he seeks a new type of epic heroism,
one no longer based on the military prowess of heroes
which dominated classical epics such as *The Aeneid*. This
new heroism is exemplified by Eve in Book X. Adam
and Eve mutually recriminate one another for causing the
Fall. Adam particularly chastises Eve as having become the
model for: 'innumerable/Disturbances on earth through
female snares' (X, 896–7). Eve, however, regains her
submissiveness. She falls humble at Adam's feet and begs

forgiveness. More importantly, she also wishes to suffer for them both:

> to the place of judgement will return,
> There with my cries importune heaven, that all
> The sentence, from thy head removed, may light
> On me, sole cause to thee of all this woe,
> Me, me only, just object of his ire.

(X, 932–6)

The result of Eve's action, Milton constantly emphasising her submissive humility, is to cause Adam's hatred to vanish and peace between the two to be restored. The conditions which prompt humanity's salvation have emerged from Eve's regaining a proper sense of her female place as subject before the male. But Eve is not the 'hero' of *Paradise Lost*. Rather, her actions emphasise the qualities of the true hero, the Messiah Christ. It will be his submissive action in abandoning his godhead and willingly suffering for mankind which indicates the greater heroism. Christ's abandonment of the masculine godhead for the feminine humanity is a greater sacrifice than Eve's desire to suffer. Not only is the scale of his act of humility greater, Christ does so without cause. Eve accepts she is 'just object' of godly anger. Messiah is the truly innocent victim.

James Grantham Turner has noted how female virtues become essential to the new definition of heroism in *Paradise Lost*.[1] The paradise within, which is the possible new condition of a reclaimed humanity, appears based on silent endurance in the private sphere. As Turner notes, ' "The mind itself", at home in the spacious circuits of her musing', bears a feminine pronoun.[2] *Paradise Lost*, thus, celebrates feminine virtues diplayed through the male Messiah and, in the post-Edenic world, it will be the male's ability to accept the feminine which will count for true heroism. Although both Adam and Eve take 'their solitary way' out of Eden, Milton's framework makes it clear that it is the male who has lost easy companionship with God. Eve reveals that, even after the Fall, Adam is everything to her: 'thou to me/Art all things under heaven, all places thou' (XII, 617–18). The woman remains somehow, 'mindless

---

[1] Ibid., esp. pp. 230–309.
[2] Ibid., p. 187.

the while'. It is the male who knowingly and heroically accepts the conditions of feminine humility and passivity. Milton's approval of positive feminine qualities appear largely confined to the males able to appropriate them.

The example of *Paradise Lost* makes it clear that negotiating gender in Renaissance writing is a complex process. Renaissance ideas of male and female categories of experience being present in both sexes complement modern psychological perspectives on the interior make-up of the psyche. Because of this, employing psychoanaltyic perspectives in the analysis of figures who are not people, who need not even be viewed as characters in any realistic sense, may, nevertheless, be seen to achieve important insights into the construction of Renaissance cultural identities. As is also apparent, though, that dominance of patriarchal attitudes appears to cause women in male-authored texts almost inevitably to be presented in reductive roles, even when female virtues are embraced.

The limited number of roles available to women are effectively confined to two types, as we see with Milton's Eve. Women are either fallen, easily tempted victims of emotionalism that outweighs reason as exemplified by the first Eve; or they resemble the second Eve, the Virgin Mary, being seen as humble, obedient and the vehicle for the male saviour, Christ. Women, therefore, are imagined either leading men to destruction or salvation. Women are perceived either hastening bodily corruption, decay and death, or promoting immortality, permanence and salvation.

The figure of the living female saint, though, is usually suspect to male Renaissance writers. It is women who have died and proceeded to a higher world, such as Donne's Elizabeth Drury of *The Anniversaries* or Crashaw's St Teresa, who are usually presented as the true ideals. Male authors are uncomfortable with the idea of direct contact with virtuous women. Their virtuous appearance, or claims about these women's ennobling powers, are frequently matched by misgivings that they are not what they seem. Beneath the apparent ideal lurks a corrupter. Virtue and its accompanying beauty are portrayed as a false mask, giving way to the misogyny which characterises Posthumous's bitter

disavowal of Imogen in *Cymbeline*. It does not take
much to convince him that she has slept with Iacomo.
A readiness to accept women as unstable is articulated
throughout male-authored writing, even in those texts
that praise women as spiritually uplifting. But it is not
simply that fears of the female corrupter inevitably
raise male paranoid anxieties. Frequently, a belief in
feminine inconstancy becomes a device for a great deal
of linguistic play, allowing the male author to depict folly,
self-deception, and emotional victimisation as a spirited
game in which men and women play (or more accurately
in which men play and women take their assigned parts).
Reducing women's roles to fit the conditions associated
with the first or second Eve, does not particularly confer
powers on females to destroy or to amend males. The
male author may use the implications of these reductive
female roles to assume control, using his belief of what
women 'really are' to his own advantage. As we saw
with Donne's playful approach to his mistress in 'Elegy
19', the male can construct fantasies of sexual possession
without responsibility.

Donne's secular love poetry abounds in a skilful manipulation of these two reductive types of female roles so
that he can gain control of women. The well-known 'The
Good Morrow' offers a prime example. Donne creates
the conditions where he proudly parades his previous
sexual conquests as mere foretastes of his supposed newly
discovered love: 'If ever any beauty I did see,/Which I
desired, and got, 'twas but a dream of thee.' And so
he suggests he has now discovered his true ideal female
in the silent figure the poem addresses, a partner who
creates the conditions of perfection, a permanent stability
and consequent immortality:

> My face in thine eye, thine in mine appears,
> And true plain hearts do in the faces rest,
> Where can we find two better hemispheres
> Without sharp north, without declining west?
> What ever dies, was not mixed equally;
> If our two loves be one, or, thou and I
> Love so alike, that none doe slacken, none can die.

The cartographic image indicates the perfection Donne
is seeking. The lovers are represented as joined spheres,

the circle traditionally symbolising the incorruptible, perfectly balanced divine elements. The lovers have neither 'sharp north', nor 'declining west' to upset their harmony. This leads to an apparent scientific axiom – death is the result of imbalances and unequal elemental mixtures. It follows, therefore, that perfectly mutal love combats human degeneracy leading to death. Donne's discovery of his ideal woman allows a paradise to be refounded. The conditions of Eden where death is absent are restored. Or so it will be, if the lovers do not die. The logic is cleverly calculated. The lovers are perfect provided they do not die, a human inevitability. Donne plays on the conventional colloquial meaning of 'die' as orgasm. In a perfect love, Donne would remain permanently joined to this woman, an eternal physical and metaphysical copulation. However, if he ejaculates and 'slackens' (the penis contracting), he dies. The love is not perfect. He has been deluded and his lover is not the source of perfection he believed. Rather than being the second Eve who would restore him to deathless Eden, she is the first Eve who causes him once more to lose Eden, draining his sexual vigour and diminishing him.

The implication of the poem is not a horrified discovery of human corruptibility because of the female. Rather, it offers the conditions where Donne can apparently legitimately leave this woman for some other. The present lover will become one more 'dream' of the ideal which the poet will presumably continue to pursue in order to discover a perfect love. This ostensibly desired love cannot exist, of course, because of the fallen human condition which is exemplified through sexual practice. The physical experiments undertaken to test the lovers' harmony will inevitably result in supposed metaphysical disappointment because the intensity of physical pleasure will confirm the lovers' imbalance. The higher love sought by the male poet can be claimed to be frustrated by the woman. Using versions of the two reductive roles for women, Donne can enjoy women sexually without implying that he is the source of lack or corruption. His male rhetoric is affirming his love, his completion. If the two loves are not alike, the poem's proposal is that the fault lies with the silent woman. The male has been misled and has the proof of his flaccid penis after sex to confirm his betrayal.

Such readings, attentive to the role of the silent woman in male-authored secular verse oppose the traditions of viewing Renaissance amorous verse as some type of generalised affirmation of human experience. Reading through gender, we become aware of masculine partiality in depicting the world. Celebrations of secular love are almost always reflections of male wit trying to cope with emotional obsession, and supposed victimisation by imagined female deceptions. These texts remain celebratory because the male author uses linguistic cleverness within the act of writing to establish dominance over the female. Women become placed within male writing, imposed on and exposed as the male ultimately wishes. As we see in Donne's 'The Good Morrow', the male poet is playing an elaborate game, creating the conditions where he can sexually enjoy a woman and then project her response to his passion as insufficient for his intellectually higher male ambitions. In supposedly praising her, he is establishing the grounds for rejecting her.

As Donne's poem instances, in most Renaissance writing, women are presented as a type of text, controlled by male discourses. They are there to be read and interpreted by imagined male readers. Margaret Cavendish proposed that men saw books as 'their crown . . . by which they rule and govern'. In the male-dominated discourses of Renaissance writing, it is our critical awareness of the feminist 'difference of view' which helps expose the subjugation of the female and the devices used to exert masculine control of discourse. The impact of feminist thought allows current readers to seek a critical 'other place', where the represented female object can be imagined differently from those perspectives of her which have been coerced and restricted by the male author's control of how the female may be written.

This type of critical examination of male-authored texts allow readings to emerge which are attentive to women's silences within a male Renaissance, and remind us that when previous generations of critics used masculine pronouns to characterise the period as an 'Age of Man', they were more precise than they intended. But exposing male assumptions about women in Renaissance texts also runs the danger that we imagine male writers wholly trapped within dominant social and cultural frameworks. As we saw with Margaret Cavendish, women writers could exploit cultural conditions. Similarly, we should not automatically imagine that male authors consciously or unconsciously accepted the commonplace implications of gender without offering alternatives or resistances.

Kathleen McLuskie reminds us that the historicity of Elizabethan drama is not simply the difference between social ideas then and those of the twentieth century, but the difference between artistic forms:

> Debates about historical ideas leave out of account the process by which ideological notions are mediated through the form of theatrical text and the extent to which playwrights are actively engaged in modifying and adapting that form – as often in the interests of novelty as in the service of more direct ideological pressure.[1]

Extending what McLuskie suggests, we should also consider how ideological ideas are themselves actively transformed through their being placed in different forms of writing. Genre works as a more active agent in influencing ideas, than is often assumed. More than a mediator of ideology, the literary form can impose on ideological notions, insisting they be rethought. This is more than a process of reception among readers engaging with ideas within generic presentations. It is also a means by which authors are empowered to rethink ideology. Genre works on the moments of production in allowing differences to emerge from dominant ideologies. It can enable the author to be more than just a force of social and cultural agency which orginates the text. Exploitation of generic conventions enables the structures which allow a re-figuring of accepted representations. The desire for novelty in form may be replicated by the wish for novelty in ideology.

The problem with claiming that authors significantly resisted gender stereotypes is discovering firm evidence of oppositions. We can never be certain that the argument mustered to support a resisting reading of a gendered subject is not the result of our own revaluing of a text as it is culturally re-enacted by us in our readings. The received possibilities of significance in a Renaissance text

[1] McLuskie, *Renaissance Dramatists*, op. cit., pp. 15–16 (see Preface, note 2).

may be recognised to have a historicity different from our own. But as we have seen throughout this book, that historicity is to some degree also the result of our selection. The received possibilities of significance must appear intelligible and communicable to us. If we recognise a Renaissance past which is different from our present, it is a past which is expected to be negotiable by our present. In trying to understand shifts in the Renaissance perception of gender, both how writers acted to naturalise their representations of gender so they appeared culturally representative and how they may have acted to oppose these representative models, we need again to remind ourselves of how our own cultural assumptions act to encode texts. Renaissance representations become our culturally inscribed examples of the past, organised and re-enacted for our needs. This may be the case if we witness texts as exemplifying sites of opposition to familiar assumptions about gender (the Renaissance as either beginning or an early stage in a teleological 'long march' toward greater cultural enlightenment about gender). It may as readily be the case if we witness Renaissance texts as sites of repressions and silences, working to confirm reductive notions of gender in order to secure male power (the Renaissance as a further instance of masculine culture's attempt to present the female in some stable archetypal order which our own age may be seen either continuing or resisting). We are not presented with an unknowable past, but we are presented with a past which may be known in different ways.

If male authors, therefore, represent women as texts to be deciphered, it is not often clear what these female texts are meant to signify. At the end of Shakespeare's *The Taming of the Shrew*, to take a famous example, Katherina discourses on the qualities and duties of a wife. This can be easily imagined to conform with the belief that the male is the site of order, the female of disorder. Her words can appear a perfect example of a woman subdued by patriarchy, forced to use the language of masculine superiority. In a terrible way Katherina, recalled by her husband to the table where the men are gathered, is performing as some type of tamed animal. It is a display of Petruchio's power that he has trained her, not only to perceive her woman's place in a male-dominated world, but to discourse on it according to the terms and images of masculine rhetorical eloquence:

> A woman move'd is like a fountain troubled –
> Muddy, ill-seeming, thick, bereft of beauty;
> And while it is so, none so dry or thirsty
> Will deign to sip or touch one drop of it.
> Thy husband is thy lord, thy life, thy keeper,
> Thy head, thy sovereign; one that cares for thee,
> And for thy maintenance commits his body
> To painful labour both by sea and land,
> To watch the night in storms, the day in cold,
> Whilst thou liest warm at home, secure and safe;
>
> (V, ii, 142–51)

Here we have exemplified male-dominated assumptions about women through the medium of metaphor within a male-controlled rhetoric. The woman is a fountain – an attractive, refreshing ornament designed to be consumed but, when disordered, quite unpalatable to the male drinker. The metaphoric analogy makes the presumptions which lie behind the imagery difficult to oppose without a direct assault on the whole system of the male dominance of language.

Other aspects of Katherina's speech, however, reveal possibilities which expose rather than confirm male illusions of power within the play. One thing the play has decidedly shown is that its male characters do not commit themselves to the 'painful labour' of land and sea. Rather, their way of securing fortune is to try to marry a rich wife. Indeed, one way to fortune for Petruchio is undertaken in this scene's demonstration of a supposed marital order, one which complies with Katherina's father's ideals. As a result of Kate's display of obedience to her husband, Petruchio gains another dowry of 20,000 crowns. The play as a whole might be said to ridicule the aspirations of a rising middle class (Katherina's proposal of the hard-working mercantile husband and the wife kept in comfort by his labour is an early iteration of a bourgeois social fantasy). How we react to Katherina's speech will, of course, depend on how she is speaking it, and, as we saw in the last chapter, this will depend on the conditions of performance. How we imagine she should speak it from the evidence of the play is not automatically apparent. As a text, Katherina cannot just be assumed to be easily read. She may be an example of commonplace male desires being given the opportunity of fulfilment through the control possible in a male-authored play. She may be bringing attention to the illusion of such desires. But it is impossible to argue confidently what original audiences made of her speech without reducing the diversity of issues the play approaches to a concentration on gender, which may be the result of our interests and not necessarily theirs. The play may equally well 'be about' illusions of social diversification, a theme taken up in the Christopher Sly episode which prefaces the play-within-the-play of 'the taming of the shrew'.

A similar instance of the difficulties of deciding whether some Renaissance writings confirm or challenge gender stereotypes is found in Webster's *The White Devil*. At one level it is possible that the play is exactly as its title suggests, about a woman whose beauty makes her appear attractive when she is actually a corrupter, a devil. On another level, the foregrounding of Vittoria as white devil may be ironic. Vittoria is no saint, but she is no different than the male aristocratic characters and clergy who populate the play. If she is a white devil, so are they and the emphasis of the play may be conceived to centre on a male corruption which tries to shift some of the responsibility for its lack of control to a female temptress. The play contains numerous examples where the injustices and corruptions of the courts the males control are shown to result from their own mishandling of those who they employ, actions which have nothing immediately to do with women.

In the play's trial scene (III, ii), Vittoria is prosecuted by Cardinal Monticelso for being complicit in the murder of her husband.[1] It is made clear she is a well-educated woman and her defence of herself is articulate and spirited in contrast to the Cardinal who declines into misogynist outbursts. But for Vittoria to possess this learning and to be so ready to defend herself in public can be said to indicate she is infamous. According to predominating ideology, a woman should be demure and domesticated, a figure who should not use eloquent oratory in the public

---

[1] Elizabeth M. Brennan (ed.), *The White Devil* in *Elizabeth and Jacobean Tragedies*, op. cit.

male world of the court. In defending herself, Vittoria is also condemning herself, for to break silence is to suggest that she is suspect as a virtuous woman. Her eloquence could be to signify her wantonness.

The trial scene is conducted in front of the resident ambassadors in Rome. Their presence has been arranged by the prosecution, as Monticelso explains:

> you know we have nought but circumstances
> To charge her with, about her husband's death;
> Their approbation therefore to the proofs
> Of her black lust shall make her infamous
> To all our neighbouring kingdoms.
>
> (III, i, 4–8)

The prosecution, therefore, envisages that Vittoria's display of herself will confirm their accusations. As a text to be interpreted by the male ambassadors, the prosecution imagines she will be read according to the convention that the eloquent woman is the suspect woman. Monticelso tries to create the conditions of discourse in the trial where this reading of her will be established.

Interestingly, it is the English ambassador who expresses reservations about this reading, recognising the bitterness of the Cardinal's attack. What this signifies is not clear. It may be that Webster is singling out the English as a better judge of this female text than, for example, his French counterpart who believes her guilt is evident. It may be that this is another example of a theatrical convention of making gentle mock of English gullibility in foreign places (as Jonson does with Sir Politic Would-Be in *Volpone*).

Are we supposed to interpret the prosecution arranging to have the ambassadors present a duplicitous manoeuvre which the play exposes, or a justified action to proclaim the White Devil's guilt? What is obvious is that, if Vittoria is presented to the ambassadors in a play-within-a-play as a text to be deciphered, she is also a character in a larger more complete play which is being presented to us to be deciphered. For us as audience, she cannot be read simply in this trial scene as her prosecutors wish because she is part of a complex discourse within the whole play-text. Intending to expose corruption in male government, Webster has, perhaps, unintentionally been the agent in fashioning a female character who it is difficult to categorise according to easy stereotypes with the result that these categories are disrupted. The suggestion that Vittoria is like her brother Flamino, a victim of a desire for social rank and the economic benefits it brings, questions assumptions about the female acting essentially through emotional instabilities. She becomes a calculating figure, driven by the same desires as men.

It is possible then that Vittoria becomes accidentally empowered as a more complex female character. The play may never have imagined undue prominence being given to the woman's part. In a male-controlled world of political and linguistic power, Vittoria's possibilities for action are limited, and Webster may have imagined he was deploying her role to bring attention to more significant issues centred on the male characters. It may be our current culture's more considered interest in gender which promotes readings of Vittoria which allow her to emerge so prominently in critical discussion. Or it may be that she did emerge in Renaissance productions as a powerful confrontation to male stereotypes because of the dramatist's interest in creating a novelty of dramatic form not because of ideological innovation. Finally, it may be that Webster was deliberately employing newly imagined possibilities in the representations of dramatic character to confront female stereotypes. The exploration of novelty in dramatic genres may have forced a recognition that the gender assumptions of earlier periods, where characterisation in drama was less socially and psychologically defined, could no longer be maintained. Changes in the dramatic forms of characterisation caused men and women to be represented differently in plays and this forced a recognition that they were different from the dominant cultural categorisations of gender inherited from the recent past. As the language and methods of dramatic representation altered under the pressures for novelty (pressures which resulted from commerical needs to satisfy audience demand), so what the dramatists believed was represented altered. The implications of gender were being rethought, because new male and female roles unexpectedly emerged from changing conditions of representation.

As both these examples from Shakespeare and Webster

reveal, reading with an awareness of gender may develop critical positions which seize on aspects of the plays as central without recognising that what gender represents may be viewed differently if the play is envisaged as possessing other centres of interest. Given our fascination with the implications of gender, we may distort the historicity of Renaissance gender by imagining it to possess centres of concern that may be the result of our unacknowledged cultural revaluation of the text's received possibilities of significance. This is, of course, not to imply anything untoward about a critical position that emphasises gender. It is, though, once more to bring attention to our need to recognise the partiality of our positions. We naturally gain enormous advantages through a detailed awareness of the implications of gender, but, paradoxically, we may also miss understanding aspects of Renaissance gender representations through this concentration of our critical attention.

The decoding of powerful male inscriptions of male superiority and female inferiority has been one of the most important tasks of feminist criticism. The challenge of the feminists' 'difference of view' to previous male critical readings of Renaissance culture has been genuinely to question what the Renaissance was and is. It has also been to teach us that the answers to these questions are even more difficult to articulate than was previously imagined.

Selected Reading

J. C. Agnew, *Worlds Apart: The Market and the Theatre in Anglo-American Thought 1550–1750* (Cambridge, Cambridge University Press, 1986).

Mikail Bakhtin, *Rabelais and His World*, Helene Iswolsky (trans.) (Cambridge, Mass., MIT Press, 1968).

Francis Barker, *The Tremulous Private Body: Essays on Subjection* (London, Methuen, 1984).

Elaine V. Beilin, *Redeeming Eve: Women Writers of the English Renaissance* (Princeton, Princeton University Press, 1987).

Martin Butler, *Theatre and Crisis 1632–1642* (Cambridge, Cambridge University Press, 1984).

Catherine Belsey, *The Subject of Tragedy: Identity and Difference in Renaissance Drama* (London, Methuen, 1985).

Phillipa Berry, *Of Chastity and Power: Elizabethan Literature and the Unmarried Queen* (London, Routledge, 1989).

James A. Boon, *Other Tribes and Other Scribes* (Cambridge, Cambridge University Press, 1982).

Michael D. Bristol, *Carnival and Theater: Plebeian Culture and The Structure of Authority in Renaissance England* (London, Methuen, 1985).

Roger Chartier *et al.*, *The Culture of Print: Power and the Uses of Print in Early Modern Europe* (Oxford, Polity Press, 1989).

Natalie Zemon Davis, *Fiction in the Archives: Pardon Tales and Their Tellers in Sixteenth-Century France* (Oxford, Polity Press, 1988).

Jonathan Dollimore, *Radical Tragedy: Religion, Ideology and Power in the Drama of Shakespeare and His Contemporaries* (Brighton, Harvester, 1984).

Jonathan Dollimore and Alan Sinfield (eds), *Political Shakespeare: New Essays in Cultural Materialism* (Manchester, Manchester University Press, 1985).

John Drakakis (ed.), *Alternative Shakespeares* (London, Methuen, 1985).

Margaret W. Ferguson, Maureen Quilligan and Nancy J. Vickers (eds), *Rewriting the Renaissance: The Discourses of Sexual Difference in Early Modern Europe* (Chicago, University of Chicago Press, 1986).

Jonathan Goldberg, *James I and the Politics of Literature:Jonson, Shakespeare, Donne and Their Contemporaries* (Baltimore, Johns Hopkins University Press, 1983).

Elspeth Graham *et al.* (eds), *Her Own Life: Autobiographical Writings by Seventeenth-Century Englishwomen* (London, Routledge, 1989).

Stephen Greenblatt, *Renaissance Self-Fashioning: From More to Shakespeare* (Chicago, University of Chicago Press, 1980).

Stephen Greenblatt, *Shakespearean Negotiations* (Oxford, Clarendon Press, 1988).

Terence Hawkes, *That Shakespeherian Rag: Essays on a Critical Process* (London, Methuen, 1986).

Thomas Healy and Jonathan Sawday (eds), *Literature and the English Civil War* (Cambridge, Cambridge University Press, 1990).

Margot Heinemann, *Puritanism and Theatre: Thomas Middleton and Opposition Drama under the Early Stuarts* (Cambridge, Cambridge University Press, 1980).

Elaine Hobby, *Virtue of Necessity: English Women's Writing 1649–88* (London, Virago, 1988).

Jean E. Howard and Marion F. O'Connor (eds), *Shakespeare Reproduced: The Text in History and Ideology* (New York, Methuen, 1987), pp. 47–67.

Mervyn James, *Society, Politics and Culture: Studies in Early Modern England* (Cambridge, Cambridge University Press, 1986).

Lisa Jardine, *Still Harping on Daughters: Women and Drama in the Age of Shakespeare* (Brighton, Harvester, 1983).

Ania Loomba, *Gender, Race, Renaissance Drama* (Manchester, Manchester University Press, 1989).

Kathleen McLuskie, *Renaissance Dramatists* (Hemel Hempstead, Harvester Wheatsheaf, 1989).

Leah S. Marcus, *Puzzling Shakespeare: Local Reading and Its Discontents* (California University Press, Berkeley, 1988).

Steven Mullaney, *The Place of the Stage: License, Play and Power in Renaissance England* (Chicago, University of Chicago Press, 1988).

David Norbrook, *Poetry and Politics in the English Renaissance* (London, Routledge and Kegan Paul, 1984).

Patricia Parker and Geoffrey Hartman, (eds), *Shakespeare and the Question of Theory* (New York, Methuen, 1985).

Patricia Parker and David Quint (eds), *Literary Theory/ Renaissance Texts,* (Baltimore, Johns Hopkins University Press, 1986).

Annabel Patterson, *Censorship and Interpretation: The Conditions of Writing and Reading in Early Modern England* (Madison, University of Wisconsin Press, 1984).

Annabel Patterson, *Shakespeare and the Popular Voice* (Cambridge, Mass., Basil Blackwell, 1989).

Kiernan Ryan, *Shakespeare* (Hemel Hempstead, Harvester Wheatsheaf, 1989).

Kevin Sharpe and Steven Zwicker (eds), *Politics of Discourse: The Literature and History of Seventeenth Century England* (Berkeley, University of California Press, 1987).

Simon Shepherd, *Marlowe and the Politics of Elizabethan Theatre* (Brighton, Harvester, 1986).

Margaret Spufford, *Small Books and Pleasant Histories: Popular Fiction and Its Readership in Seventeenth Century England* (London, Methuen, 1981).

Peter Stallybrass and Allon White, *The Poetics and Politics of Transgression* (London, Methuen, 1986).

H. Aram Veeser (ed.), *The New Historicism* (New York, Routledge, 1989).

Hayden White, *The Content of the Form: Narrative Discourse and Historical Representation* (Baltimore, Johns Hopkins University Press, 1987).

Index

Hyde, Edward Earl of Clarendon, 13

Jacobus, Mary, 147
James VI and I, 113, 161
James, Mervyn, 58
James, Thomas, 111
Jardine, Lisa, 3, 6
Jonson, Ben, 41–42, 49, 111–112, 116, 120, 122, 131, 176
Jordan, Constance, 150
Joyce, James, 3

Kahn, Coppelia, 147–148, 157
Knowles, James, 6

Lacan, Jacques, 149
Latimer, Hugh, 75
Lever, J. W., 141
Lovelace, Richard, 41
Lyly, John, 139

McLuskie, Kathleen, 3, 6, 172
Machiavelli, Niccolo, 138
Marcus, Laura, 6
Marlowe, Christopher, 110, 117–120, 125, 162–164
Marvell, Andrew, 12–13, 17–18, 22, 41
May, Thomas, 41
Middleton, Thomas, 113, 159–160
Miles, Robert, 6
Milton, John, ix, 12–13, 17–23, 28–29, 41, 54, 109, 112, 131, 153, 164–168
Montrose, Louis, 61, 66–69, 74
More, Sir Thomas, 58–59
Mullaney, Steven, 113–114

Norbrook, David, 102

Olivier, Sir Laurence, 7–8
Ovid, 154, 163

Parker, William Riley, 18
Parr, Tony, 6
Patterson, Annabel, 48
Plato, 87
Puttenham, George, 29–30

Rabelais, Francois, 130, 132
Ralegh, Sir Walter, 48, 93
Rich, Barnabe, 104
Rich, Penelope, 31, 33
Richard III, 56–59
Roche, Thomas P. Jr, ix
Rose, Jacqueline, 148

Samuel, Raphael, 81–82
Sawday, Jonathan, 6
Shakespeare, William, ix, 3, 7–9, 17–18, 33, 38–40, 45–48, 73–75, 77–78, 106, 111–112, 114, 116, 120–123, 132–133, 136–140, 163, 173, 177
Shaldon, Christopher, 6
Shalins, Marshall, 64–65, 71
Sharkey, Sabina, 6
Sidney, Sir Philip, 28, 30–33, 47–48, 52, 152, 164
Sinfield, Alan, 61
Smith, Stan, 6
Spenser, Edmund, ix, 48–49, 54–55, 60, 84–105, 107–109, 111–112, 127, 161, 164
Stafford, Henry Duke of Buckingham, 58
Stanley, Henry, 77
Stanley, Thomas, 41
Steiner, George, 39

Thatcher, Margaret, 85
Thucydides, 76
Tillyard, E.M.W., 7–10, 40, 143
Trapnel, Anna, 53–55
Turner, James Grantham, 167

Vaughan, Henry, 41
Virgil, 162